ASSASSINS

ASSASSINS

MUSIC AND LYRICS BY
STEPHEN SONDHEIM

BOOK BY
JOHN WEIDMAN

THEATRE COMMUNICATIONS GROUP · 1991

This publication is made possible in part with public funds from the New York State
Council on the Arts, a State Agency.

TCG books are exclusively distributed to the book trade by Consortium Book Sales and
Distribution.

Library of Congress Cataloging-in-Publication Data
Sondheim, Stephen
    [Assassins. Libretto]
    Assassins / music and lyrics by Stephen Sondheim: book by John Weidman.— IST ed.
    Libretto.
    ISBN-13: 978-1-55936-038-8 (pbk.)
    ISBN-13: 978-1-55936-039-5 (cloth)
    ISBN-10: 1-55936-038-0 (pbk.)
    ISBN-10: 1-55936-039-9 (cloth)
    1. Musicals—Librettos. 2. Presidents United States—Assassination—Drama.
    I. Weidman, John, 1946- . II. Title.
    Ml50.705a7 1991 <Case>
    782.1'4'0268—dc20   91-4809   CIP
                                                                    MN

Cover art copyright © 1991 by Neal Pozner
All photographs copyright © 1991 by Martha Swope

Design and composition by The Sarabande Press

Frontispiece: Scene Eight, Leon Czologsz (Terrence Mann) at the Temple of Music
Pavillion at the Pan-American Exposition, Buffalo, New York, September 6, 1991.

First Edition, September 1991
Eighth Printing, February 2008

Assassins was first presented by Playwrights Horizons (André Bishop, artistic director, Paul S. Daniels, executive director) in New York City, January 27, 1991. Set by Loren Sherman, costumes by William Ivey Long, lighting by Paul Gallo, choreography by D. J. Giagni, musical direction by Paul Gemignani and direction by Jerry Zaks. The cast was as follows:

LEON CZOLGOSZ	*Terrence Mann*
JOHN HINCKLEY	*Greg Germann*
CHARLES GUITEAU	*Jonathan Hadary*
GIUSEPPE ZANGARA	*Eddie Korbich*
SAMUEL BYCK	*Lee Wilkof*
LYNETTE ("SQUEAKY") FROMME	*Annie Golden*
SARA JANE MOORE	*Debra Monk*
JOHN WILKES BOOTH	*Victor Garber*
BALLADEER	*Patrick Cassidy*
EMMA GOLDMAN	*Lyn Greene*
LEE HARVEY OSWALD	*Jace Alexander*

With: *Joy Franz, John Jellison, Marcus Olson, William Parry* and *Michael Shulman.*

Assassins is based on an idea by Charles Gilbert, Jr.

PREFACE

Assassins opened at Playwrights Horizons in the middle of the Persian Gulf War. At the time we didn't know if this would help the show by delivering nightly audiences who were stirred up and willing to be stirred up even further, or hurt it because people were feeling patriotic and scared and might not want to see something that presented a darkly comic vision of the killing off of a number of American Presidents.

In retrospect, I don't feel that the war had much to do with the show's critical reception (mostly negative) or with its relatively brief run, although I'm sure that in years to come people will blame the show's supposed failure (i.e., brief run) on its unfortunate timing, just as history tends to blame the "failure" of other New York shows on newspaper strikes or blizzards.

I know that for those of us who worked on *Assassins* the show was a triumph. We believed in it, and were surprised and heartened by the enthusiasm of audiences and by the long lines of people waiting for ticket cancellations every night.

What is *Assassins* about? Well, I urge you to go straight to the prologue and find out. That first scene does what most first scenes do in a good musical—it introduces the characters and sets up the tone and themes of the show. The no-man's land of a carnival in which all the assassins are given their guns and their targets, together with the shocking lyric, "C'mere and kill a President," certainly sets the evening up, and as the assassins sing of their (and everyone's) right to be happy and have their dreams, one has a sense of an America whose extraordinary freedom has created a land where accidents of all kinds can happen. Any kid can grow up to be President; any kid can grow up to be his killer.

People have asked if the show changed a lot during its long preview period—actually, it didn't change much at all. Lyrics were polished, the character of the Balladeer was clarified somewhat, one or two numbers were restaged, and so on. The only area of uncertainty was the opening number I just described. A lot of people, including fainthearted me, were nervous about the opening number, nervous that people might be offended in the first five minutes. During rehearsals, Sondheim wrote a beautiful patriotic anthem to be sung by a crowd of excited people waiting for a Presidential motorcade to go by; one by one the assassins slip into this crowd and the inevitable happens. But the "Flag Song," as it was called, seemed soft, and the authors wisely stuck to their original plans.

Reading a play, especially a musical play, is not the same as seeing it. Because most of you who are reading this did not have a chance to see *Assassins*, I would like to describe some of my favorite moments and images:

- The charming scene between Emma Goldman and a tremulous Leon Czolgosz when he declared his love. I will always remember the look on Terry Mann's face, and the moment when he helped Lyn Greene carry her suitcase. The scene, which in a conventional musical would surely have had some kind of bittersweet ballad at the end of it, always got applause—for the unaffected sincerity of the writing and the playing.

- An out-of-the-body shriek: Jonathan Hadary as Charles Guiteau reaching the top of a scaffold, a noose around his neck, and defiantly yelling into the void, "I shall be remembered!", his eyes bulging, his body shaking.

- The series of beautiful, ghostly, heartbreaking musical wails that preceded "Another National Anthem." The set's turntable revolved, the assassins stepped off it one by one, and images of the Stars and Stripes were projected onto the screen behind them. Perfection.

- The ferocity with which the assassins turned on the Balladeer and then on the audience as they spat out the last chorus of "Another National Anthem," and Lee Wilkof's look of leering contempt at the end of it as he exited singing, "Sure, the mailman won the lottery. . . " Not only did it seem as if he had turned on us; it was as if he had turned on the song as well.

- The moment late in the show when the Dallas Book Depository set was revealed—the only completely detailed setting in a spare, abstract design—and we saw a thin figure in a T-shirt and jeans staring sullenly out the window, listening to country-and-western music. We realized that this was Lee Harvey Oswald, and that there would be a Kennedy scene after all. This moment inevitably evoked gasps of surprise and occasionally horror. And I remember another moment, later still, when Oswald decided to join the assassins. Booth asked, "Why do these rednecks always have three names? James Earl Ray! John Wilkes Booth—!" and Oswald, *timidly* if you please, piped up almost like Oliver Twist asking for more gruel, "Lee Harvey Oswald!"

This entire scene, in fact, with its surreal vision of what might have happened that terrible day in Dallas, thrilled and terrified night after night. Watching Jace Alexander as Oswald aim his rifle out the window and shoot, hearing the earsplitting musical chords that followed as he lurched, dazed and defiant, out of the room . . . it was almost unbearable.

Of course, there was a lot of laughter within the revue/vaudeville/musical comedy scheme of the play, and if I most remember the darker moments it's only because *Assassins*, if for nothing else but its subject matter, is a dark piece. Some people said, their eyebrows raised to the heavens, "Oh, you can't do a show about those killers. It's a taboo subject in America." Others felt, before they saw the show or because they didn't see the show, that it glorified assassination; others were overwhelmed. The chief criticism we heard was that the show had no point of view; how could you write a show about people who kill Presidents and not have a point of view?

Well, if Sondheim and Weidman didn't have a point of view, why the hell did they write it in the first place? To answer, let me quote from something John Weidman wrote recently:

> Thirteen people have tried to kill the President of the United States. Four have succeeded. These murderers and would-be murderers are generally dismissed as maniacs and misfits who have little in common with each other, and nothing in common with the rest of us.
>
> *Assassins* suggests otherwise. *Assassins* suggests that while these individuals are, to say the least, peculiar—taken as a group they are peculiarly *American*. And that behind the variety of motives which they articulated for their murderous outbursts, they share a common purpose: a desperate desire to reconcile intolerable feelings of impotence with an inflamed and malignant sense of entitlement.
>
> Why do these dreadful events happen *here*, with such horrifying frequency, and in such an appallingly similar fashion? *Assassins* suggests it is because we live in a country

whose most cherished national myths, at least as currently propagated, encourage us to believe that in America our dreams not only *can* come true, but *should* come true, and that if they don't someone or something is to blame.

We are accustomed, in our musical theatre, to examining the lives of those Americans who reveal to us the best part of who we are: John Adams, Benjamin Franklin, George M. Cohan. Sondheim and Weidman set themselves a different task. And what they succeeded in doing, brilliantly, was to humanize these assassins in a series of vignettes, sketches, set pieces and ballads, and thereby to allow us to get into their minds. Their individual stories, part fiction and mostly fact, were presented on stage for us to see, and seeing America through the stories of its villains, instead of its heroes, was an unsettling and unusual experience.

At the end of one of the performances, an audience member said to his companion, "I liked it, but who are you supposed to feel for?" She replied, her eyes filled with tears, "Us. You're supposed to feel for us." And that was the power of this show: you went out into the night thinking how much you loved your country despite how troubled it had become, and you felt happy and sad to be an American.

It's hard to write about a show that so few people actually saw, but it is my hope that the publication of this book and the appearance of the wonderfully vibrant original cast recording will give birth to other productions. I know that for Playwrights Horizons *Assassins* is one of the best things we've ever done. The show touched a nerve, God knows, and it did so in a funny, daring, high wire-act way. Sondheim, Weidman and their talented colleagues created something amazing. The show will live on.

André Bishop
Playwrights Horizons
June, 1991

ASSASSINS

NOTE ON SLIDES

The scenic design of *Assassins* as it was presented at
Playwrights Horizons in New York City relied heavily
on the use of slides and projections. Some were
projections of period engravings or photographs
depicting Presidents, assassins, or assassinations. Others
simply set the scene: The Pan-American Exposition in
Buffalo; a public park. This script describes several of
these slides in order to give some sense of the way in
which they were used. But slides and projections should
not be looked upon as the only way, or even necessarily
the best way, to meet the scenic challenges which the
musical presents.

CAST OF CHARACTERS

JOHN WILKES BOOTH (1838–1865). Assassinated
President Abraham Lincoln during a performance of
"Our American Cousin" at Ford's Theater, Washington,
D.C., April 14, 1865.

CHARLES GUITEAU (1841–1882). Assassinated President
James Garfield in the waiting room of the Baltimore &
Potomac Railroad Station, Washington, D.C., July 2,
1881.

LEON CZOLGOSZ (1873–1901). Assassinated President
William McKinley during a public reception at the
Temple of Music Pavilion at the Pan-American
Exposition, Buffalo, New York, September 6, 1901.

GIUSEPPE ZANGARA (1900–1933). Attempted to
assassinate President-elect Franklin D. Roosevelt as
Roosevelt greeted well-wishers in Bayfront Park, Miami,
Florida, February 15, 1933.

SAMUEL BYCK (1930–1974). Attempted to assassinate
President Richard Nixon; hijacked a commercial jetliner
which he intended to crash dive into the White House,
Baltimore-Washington International Airport, February
22, 1974.

LYNETTE ("SQUEAKY") FROMME (1948–). Attempted to assassinate President Gerald Ford as he left the Senator Hotel, Sacramento, California, September 5, 1975.

SARA JANE MOORE (1930–). Attempted to assassinate President Gerald Ford as he left the St. Francis Hotel, San Francisco, California, September 22, 1975.

JOHN HINCKLEY (1955–). Attempted to assassinate President Ronald Reagan as he left the Washington Hilton, Washington, D.C., March 30, 1981.

LEE HARVEY OSWALD (1939–1963). Assassinated President John F. Kennedy from the sixth floor of the Texas School Book Depository, Dallas, Texas, November 22, 1963.

THE BALLADEER. A Woody Guthrie/Pete Seeger-style folk singer.

EMMA GOLDMAN. Turn-of-the-century anarchist agitator and feminist.

THE PROPRIETOR of a shooting gallery at a carnival.

DAVID HEROLD. One of John Wilkes Booth's confederates; aided Booth in his attempted escape.

A BARTENDER.

SARA JANE MOORE'S NINE-YEAR-OLD SON, BILLY.

PRESIDENTS JAMES GARFIELD AND GERALD FORD.

VARIOUS REPORTERS, PHOTOGRAPHERS, TOURISTS, BYSTANDERS, etc.

SCENE 1

A Shooting Gallery in a fairground.

Flashing lights—red, white and blue. Dimly seen target figures, all men, dressed formally in various fashions from the last two hundred years, trundle by on a conveyor belt.

A shelf of prizes, filled with the usual stuffed animals, small dolls and souvenirs, plus a sexy life-size doll, money, elaborate scrolled documents, books, newspapers with large but unreadable headlines, and fancy jars of colored liquid.

American eagles and dusty Presidential seals range along the top border of the booth.

A Proprietor stands behind the counter, idly picking his teeth. Calliope music.

Music changes to a slow, disgruntled beat. A scruffy sullen laborer, Leon Czolgosz, a man in his late twenties, shuffles in disconsolately, paring an apple or eating a sausage, looking at the ground.

PROPRIETOR *(Sings)*:
  Hey, pal—feelin' blue?
  Don't know what to do?
  Hey, pal—

(Czolgosz looks up)

I mean you—
Yeah.
C'mere and kill a President.

(Proprietor reaches under the counter, pushes a button; a sign lights up: HIT THE "PREZ" AND WIN A PRIZE. *Czolgosz stops, shuffles over)*

No job? Cupboard bare?
One room, no one there?
Hey, pal, don't despair—
You wanna shoot a President?

(Puts a gun in Czolgosz's hand)

C'mon and shoot a President . . .

(Czolgosz stares at the gun)

Some guys
Think they can't be winners.

(Smiles, shakes his head)

First prize
Often goes to rank beginners.

CZOLGOSZ *(Speaks with an accent)*: How much?
PROPRIETOR: Four-fifty.

(As Czolgosz hesitates)

Iver-Johnson, .32. Rubber handle. Owls stamped on the sides.
CZOLGOSZ: All right, give me.

(Czolgosz fishes out the money, pays; Proprietor hands him the gun, which he slowly examines; meanwhile John Hinckley, a soft plump twenty-one-year-old, ambles aimlessly on)

PROPRIETOR *(To Hinckley)*:
Hey, kid, failed your test?
Dream girl unimpressed?
Show her you're the best.

6

(Proffers another kind of gun)

If you can shoot a President—

(Hinckley approaches the counter listlessly)

You can get the prize
With the big blue eyes . . .

(Indicates the sexy doll)

Skinny little thighs
And those big blue eyes . . .

(Presses the gun into Hinckley's hand; Czolgosz, continuing to examine his gun, tries unsuccessfully to break it open)

CZOLGOSZ *(To Proprietor)*: Mister—

PROPRIETOR *(Ignoring him; encouragingly, to Hinckley)*:
Everybody's
Got the right
To be happy.
Don't stay mad,
Life's not as bad
As it seems.
If you keep your
Goal in sight,
You can climb to
Any height.
Everybody's
Got the right
To their dreams . . .

HINCKLEY: Deal.

(Hinckley reaches for money; calliope music resumes)

CZOLGOSZ: Mister—

(Proprietor pauses)

HINCKLEY *(Plunking money down on counter)*: I said "deal."

7

CZOLGOSZ *(To Hinckley)*: You. Wait your turn.

HINCKLEY: It is my turn.

CZOLGOSZ: I was here first—

PROPRIETOR: Watch it now, no violence!

(Proprietor shows Czolgosz how his gun opens and closes; Czolgosz and Hinckley freeze as Charles Guiteau enters: quick, furtive, seedy but dapper, in a clean white shirt, but otherwise all in black, including a broad-brimmed black felt hat pulled rather low; thick scraggly black beard and intense eyes, his scruffy shoes highly polished, but with no socks underneath)

Hey, fella,
Feel like you're a failure?
Bailiff on your tail? Your
Wife run off for good?
Hey, fella,
Feel misunderstood?
C'mere and kill a President . . .

GUITEAU: Okay!

(Guiteau approaches the booth brightly and, during the following, pays the Proprietor, who hands him a silver-mounted .44, which he proceeds to play with ostentatiously. At the same time, Giuseppe Zangara, a tiny angry man, enters, groans and leans against the side of the counter, rubbing his stomach)

ZANGARA: Marron . . .

PROPRIETOR *(In stage Italian)*:
What's-a wrong, boy?
Boss-a treat you crummy?
Trouble with you tummy?
This-a bring you some relief.

(Holds out gun)

Here, give some
Hail-a to da Chief—

8

(Guiteau freezes; music continues under)

ZANGARA: You gimme prize—

PROPRIETOR *(Waves his arm)*: Anything you want.

ZANGARA *(Trying to reach over the counter)*: I want prize. You gimme prize!

PROPRIETOR *(Pulls him back; Zangara reaches for the gun, but Proprietor lifts it up high)*: Only eight bucks. Cheap for "anything you want."

(Sings front, as Zangara pays for the gun, grabs it and examines it furiously)

Everybody's
Got the right
To be different,

(Samuel Byck, a fattish greasy man in a sweat-marked Santa Claus suit, enters and parades by, carrying a sign which reads: SANTA SAYS, ALL I WANT FOR CHRISTMAS IS MY CONSTITU-TIONAL RIGHT [OVER]*)*

Even though
At times they go
To extremes.
Aim for what you
Want a lot—
Everybody
Gets a shot.

(Byck reverses direction, revealing the other side of his sign: TO PEACEABLY PETITION MY GOVERNMENT FOR THE REDRESS OF MY GRIEVANCES*)*

Everybody's
Got the right
To their dreams—

(Zangara freezes with his gun; music continues; Byck puts the sign down, goes to the counter. As he pays for and receives a gun

9

from the Proprietor, Lynette Fromme, a small, intense girl swathed in red religious robes, enters sullenly and crosses slowly, eyeing the Shooting Gallery with interest. At the same time, Sara Jane Moore, a bright-eyed, heavy-set middle-aged woman, enters from the other side of the stage and moves toward the booth with cheery curiosity, fishing clumsily in her handbag for money. As Fromme approaches the counter, Guiteau glances at her roguishly, to no avail. Proprietor continues to Fromme, as she approaches)

Yo, baby!
Looking for a thrill?

(Points off)

The Ferris wheel is that way.

(Fromme, impassive, comes closer)

No, baby,
This requires skill—

(Fromme slams money down with a bang; Proprietor shrugs, gives her a gun)

Okay, you want to give it a try . . .

(As Fromme plays with the gun, aiming it, feeling it, practicing to draw it from under her skirt, Moore is spilling keys, credit cards, lipstick, etc., all over the counter next to Czolgosz. Proprietor waves her away)

Jeez, lady—!

(Indicates Czolgosz)

Give the guy some room!

(Points off)

The bumper cars are that way . . .

(Moore finds her money and drops it in his hand; reluctantly, he gives her a .38, which she accidentally points at his stomach)

Please, lady—

(Turning the barrel away)

Don't forget that guns can go boom . . .

(Fromme, Guiteau and Moore freeze with their guns; music changes to the slow, faintly sinister vamp that we heard at the beginning. John Wilkes Booth enters, handsome and thoughtful, theatrically but elegantly dressed in black. He contemplates the scene. After a beat the Proprietor and the Assassins slowly turn and look at him. It is clear that all of them, even the Proprietor, view him with a certain deference)

(Proprietor continues softly)

Hey, gang,
Look who's here.
There's our
Pioneer.

(To Booth)

Hey, chief,

(Gesturing towards the Assassins)

Loud and clear:

(During the following, the Proprietor winds among the Assassins, distributing ammunition)

BOOTH *(To the Assassins)*:
Everybody's
Got the right
To be happy.
Say, "Enough!"
It's not as tough
As it seems.

Don't be scared
You won't prevail,
Everybody's
Free to fail,
No one can be put in jail
For his dreams.

*(During the following, the Assassins load their guns in a stylized
way, perhaps inserting the bullets rhythmically)*

Free country—!

PROPRIETOR:
—Means your dreams can come true:

BOOTH:
Be a scholar—

PROPRIETOR:
Make a dollar—

BOOTH, PROPRIETOR:
Free country—!

BOOTH:
—Means they listen to *you*:

PROPRIETOR:
Scream and holler—

BOOTH:
Grab 'em by the collar!

BOOTH, PROPRIETOR:
Free country—!

BOOTH:
—Means you don't have to sit—

PROPRIETOR:
That's it!

BOOTH:
—And put up with the shit.

(All turn front, loaded guns at their sides, shuffling toward us)

GROUP *(High voices)*:
Everybody's
Got the right
To some sunshine—

BOOTH:
Everybody . . .

GROUP *(Low voices)*:
Not the sun,
But maybe one
Of its beams.

ALL:
Rich man, poor man,
Black or white,
Pick your apple,
Take a bite,
Everybody
Just hold tight
To your dreams.
Everybody's
Got the right
To their dreams . . .

(As they hold the note, they turn slowly upstage to face the targets, raising their guns. Just as they are about to aim and shoot, we hear "Hail to the Chief" played by a military band, then a voice on the P.A. system)

VOICE: Ladies and Gentlemen, the President of the United States, Abraham Lincoln!

(Booth looks up at an imaginary theatre box; the Assassins turn front and follow his gaze)

13

BOOTH *(To one of the Assassins)*: Excuse me.

(Booth exits. A gunshot offstage—BANG!)

BOOTH'S VOICE: Sic Semper Tyrannis!

(Booth's cry echoes and reverberates as . . .)

SCENE 2

A Balladeer, a twentieth-century folk singer, enters carrying a guitar (or mandolin or banjo). Behind him a slide is projected: a nineteenth-century engraving of Booth assassinating Lincoln.

BALLADEER *(Strums a chord, sings)*:
Someone tell the story,

(Strums another)

Someone sing the song.

(Two more)

Every now and then
The country
Goes a little wrong.

(Continues strumming)

Every now and then
A madman's
Bound to come along.
Doesn't stop the story—
Story's pretty strong.
Doesn't change the song . . .

(Music changes to a lively folk style. Slide disappears as lights come up on a tobacco barn in rural Virginia. It is the middle of the night. Scattered about are blankets, saddle bags, the remains of a hurried meal, and a pair of roughhewn crutches. Booth sits huddled

15

on the floor, wet and trembling, a shawl pulled around his shoul-ders. He is taking long pulls at a brandy bottle and reading feverishly through a pile of newspapers)

Johnny Booth was a handsome devil,
Got up in his rings and fancy silks.
Had him a temper, but kept it level.
Everybody called him Wilkes.

Why did you do it, Johnny?
Nobody agrees.
You who had everything,
What made you bring
A nation to its knees?

Some say it was your voice had gone,
Some say it was booze.
They say you killed a country, John,
Because of bad reviews.

Johnny lived with a grace and glitter,
Kinda like the lives he lived on stage.
Died in a barn, in pain and bitter,
Twenty-seven years of age.

Why did you do it, Johnny,
Throw it all away?
Why did you do it, boy,
Not just destroy
The pride and joy
Of Illinois,
But all the U.S.A?

Your brother made you jealous, John,
You couldn't fill his shoes.
Was that the reason, tell us, John—
Along with bad reviews?

(Music continues under, the Balladeer humming or softly whistling the tune. Booth hurls one of the newspapers aside)

BOOTH: *Damn!*

(He takes a tattered diary out of his pocket and starts to write. The door bangs open and David Herold rushes in; music stops)

HEROLD: They're coming! They'll be here any minute!

(Herold begins frantically gathering their things. Booth throws down his pen; his hand is trembling)

BOOTH: I need your help.

HEROLD *(Handing him the crutches)*: Here—

BOOTH: Not with those! I've got to write this and I can't hold the pen!

HEROLD: Johnny, they've found us! We've got to get out of here!

BOOTH: Not till I finish this.

HEROLD: *Johnny—*

BOOTH: *No!* Have you seen these papers?! Do you know what they're calling me?! A common cutthroat! A hired assassin! This one says I'm mad!

HEROLD: We must have been mad to think we could kill the President and get away with it!

BOOTH: We *did* get away with it! He was a bloody tyrant and we brought him down! And I will not have history think I did it for a bag of gold or in some kind of rabid fit!

HEROLD: Johnny, we have to go—

BOOTH: No! I have to make my case. And I need you to take it down.

(Booth holds out the diary and the pen)

HEROLD: We don't have time—

(Booth draws his gun, aims it at Herold)

BOOTH: *Take it down.*

(A beat. Herold takes the pen and the diary. Booth starts to dictate. Herold writes)

17

An indictment. Of the former President of the United States, Abraham Lincoln, who is herein charged with the following High Crimes and Misdemeanors—

BALLADEER *(Sings)*:
They say your ship was sinkin', John . . .

BOOTH *(Glances at Balladeer briefly; back to Herold)*: One: That you did ruthlessly provoke a war between the States which cost some six hundred thousand of my countrymen their lives. Two—

BALLADEER:
You'd started missing cues . . .

BOOTH *(Glances again; back to Herold)*: *Two*: That you did silence your critics in the North by hurling them into prison without benefit of charge or trial. Three—

BALLADEER:
They say it wasn't Lincoln, John.

BOOTH *(To Balladeer)*: Shut up! *Three*—

BALLADEER:
You'd merely had
A slew of bad
Reviews—

BOOTH: I said *shut up!*

(The door opens, revealing a Union Soldier; Booth whirls and shoots—BANG! The Soldier screams and falls back)

HEROLD: What are we going to do?!
BOOTH: We're going to finish this. Three—
VOICE FROM OUTSIDE BARN: Booth! I have fifty soldiers out here, Booth! Give yourselves up or we'll set fire to the barn!
HEROLD: Don't shoot! I'm coming out!

(Herold throws down the diary and rushes out the door)

BOOTH: *No*—!

(Booth lunges for Herold and collapses, clutching his broken leg. A beat. He retrieves the diary, turns to the Balladeer)

I have given up my life for one act, you understand? Do not let history rob me of its meaning. Pass on the truth! You're the only one who can. Please . . .

(Booth tosses the diary to the Balladeer. He glances at it without opening it, as if he knew the contents)

BALLADEER *(Front)*:
   He said,
   "Damn you, Lincoln,
   You had your way—

BOOTH:
   Tell them, boy!

BALLADEER:
   With blood you drew out
   Of Blue and Gray!"

BOOTH:
   Tell it all!
   Tell them till they listen!

BALLADEER:
   He said,
   "Damn you, Lincoln,
   And damn the day
   You threw the 'U' out
   Of U.S.A.!"

   He said:

BOOTH:
   Hunt me down, smear my name,
   Say I did it for the fame,
   What I did was kill the man who killed my country.

Now the Southland will mend,
Now this bloody war can end,
Because someone slew the tyrant
Just as Brutus slew the tyrant—

BALLADEER:
He said:

BALLADEER, BOOTH *(Front)*:
Damn you, Lincoln,
You righteous whore!

BOOTH *(To Balladeer)*:
Tell 'em!
Tell 'em what he did!

BALLADEER, BOOTH *(Front)*:
You turned your spite into civil war!

BOOTH *(To Balladeer)*:
Tell 'em!
Tell 'em the truth!

BALLADEER:
And more . . .

BOOTH:
Tell 'em, boy—
Tell 'em how it happened,
How the end doesn't mean that it's over,
How surrender is not the end!
Tell them:

(Quiet and plaintive)

How the country is not what it was,
Where there's blood on the clover,
How the nation can never again
Be the hope that it was.

How the bruises may never be healed,
How the wounds are forever,
How we gave up the field
But we still wouldn't yield,

(Building in anger)

How the Union can never recover
From that vulgar,
High and mighty
Niggerlover,
Never—!

(Regaining control)

Never. Never. Never.
No, the country is not what it was . . .

(The sound of crackling flames. Smoke begins to seep under the walls of the barn. As music continues under, Booth bows his head and prays silently; after a moment, he sings softly)

. . . Damn my soul if you must,
Let my body turn to dust,
Let it mingle with the ashes of the country.

Let them curse me to hell,
Leave it to history to tell:
What I did, I did well,
And I did it for my country.

Let them cry, "Dirty traitor!"
They will understand it later—
The country is not what it was . . .

(He draws his gun, puts it to his head. Blackout on Booth. A gunshot—BANG!)

(The Balladeer strums and sings)

BALLADEER:

Johnny Booth was a headstrong fellow,
Even he believed the things he said.
Some called him noble, some said yellow.
What he was was off his head.

How could you do it, Johnny,
Calling it a cause?
You left a legacy
Of butchery
And treason we
Took eagerly,
And thought you'd get applause.

But traitors just get jeers and boos,
Not visits to their graves,
While Lincoln, who got mixed reviews,
Because of you, John, now gets only raves.

Damn you, Johnny!
You paved the way
For other madmen
To make us pay.
Lots of madmen
Have had their say—
But only for a day.

Listen to the stories.
Hear it in the songs.
Angry men
Don't write the rules,
And guns don't right the wrongs.

Hurts a while,
But soon the country's

Back where it belongs,
And that's the truth.

Still and all . . .

Damn you, Booth!

(Music continues, as he disappears)

SCENE 3

A turn of the century saloon. It could be on 14th Street in 1900, or on Columbus Avenue in 1991.

Sitting at the bar are John Hinckley and Leon Czolgosz. Czolgosz is staring into a shot glass of whiskey. Hinckley is listlessly eating peanuts. On the bar in front of him are several Coke bottles and a pile of money, his change from the Bartender, who is lazily wiping glasses. Sitting at a table by himself, scowling and clutching a glass of buttermilk, is Giuseppe Zangara. Booth sits at another table, reading a copy of Variety.

Samuel Byck, who has just entered, stands at the bar, breathing heavily and sweating. He wears his Santa Claus suit. His picket sign leans against the bar. He unhooks his Santa beard and wipes his face with it.

Zangara's stomach growls. He grimaces in pain. No one reacts. Byck beckons to the Bartender.

BYCK: Glass of water.

(The Bartender serves the water; Byck gulps it down)

Has Dick Nixon been in today?

BARTENDER: Who?

BYCK: President Richard Nixon.

BARTENDER: We don't get many Presidents in here, pal.

BYCK: If he comes in, call me. I'll be across the street.

(Byck picks up his sign and starts out. Charles Guiteau strides in. He stops, grins at Byck's Santa Claus suit)

GUITEAU: Fa, la, la, la, la—la, la, la, la!

BYCK: Fuck you.

(Byck goes out. Guiteau steps up to the bar)

GUITEAU: Morning! Morning, all! Barkeep, your wine list, please.

BARTENDER: We got beer and whiskey.

GUITEAU: Very well, I'll have beer and whiskey! In fact, we'll all have beer and whiskey! Drinks for everyone!

(Guiteau beams at Czolgosz and Hinckley, who ignore him. The Bartender starts doing figures on his order pad; Guiteau plucks a $50 bill off Hinckley's pile of change and holds it up)

Who is that? I can't quite make him out.

HINCKLEY: Ulysses S. Grant.

GUITEAU: Marvelous President! No need to assassinate a President like that! Why, if Grant had been re-nominated I would not have been compelled to remove that scoundrel who succeeded him, James Garfield—

BARTENDER: That's gonna be eight-fifty.

GUITEAU *(Handing him the $50 bill)*: Keep the change!

(The Bartender starts to serve the drinks. Zangara's stomach growls again. Booth lowers his paper)

BOOTH: You know, you really ought to do something about that stomach.

ZANGARA: I do everything about this stomach!

BOOTH: Oh, yes?

ZANGARA: I give up wine! No good! I give up smokes! No good! I quit my work! No good! I move Miami! No good! I take appendix out! No good! Nothing, no good! *Nothing! Nothing! Nothing!*

BOOTH: Have you considered shooting Franklin Roosevelt?

25

ZANGARA: You think that help?
BOOTH: It couldn't hurt.

(Zangara nods, slaps money on the table, and stalks out. The Bartender sets a beer mug and a shot glass in front of Guiteau. Guiteau raises the glass)

GUITEAU: Gentlemen, a toast! To the Presidency of the United States. An office which by its mere existence reassures us that the possibilities of life are limitless. An office the mere idea of which reproaches us when we fall short of being all that we can be. A grand and glorious office to which at least one among us may one day aspire. Gentlemen, what can I say? *Hail to the Chief!*

(He drains his glass; no one pays any attention. To Hinckley:)

What did you think?

(Hinckley stares at him)

The toast. How did you find it? Stirring? Inspirational?
HINCKLEY: I guess—
GUITEAU: Then perhaps you'd like to buy a copy of my book! It isn't much, some random musings on the mysteries of Creation— *(Whipping a small book out of his breast pocket)* "The Truth," by Charles Guiteau!

(He holds the book out to Hinckley, who reaches for it and knocks one of the bottles off the bar—CRASH!)

CZOLGOSZ: *Stupid boy!*
HINCKLEY: It's just a bottle, man. Somebody'll clean it up.
CZOLGOSZ: And somebody will have to make another one!
HINCKLEY: So?
CZOLGOSZ: So? I tell you "so!" *(Snatching one of Hinckley's empty bottles)* You see this? You ever ask yourself, how did this come to be? I tell you how. In the factory where I work there is an oven. Inside the oven, there are bottles. Cooking. I stand at the oven door. The door is open. Twelve hundred

degrees. I hold my breath. If I breathe in, my insides cook like the bottles. A bell rings and I reach into the oven. I wear gloves. Inside the gloves my hands are rubbed with grease and wrapped in rags. But still each time my hands begin to burn. I take the bottles out. I carry them across the room. Just so. If two bottles touch, they break. The burning pieces fall on me, my hair, my clothes. From this I have this mark— *(He pulls down the collar of his shirt)* Will always be like this. From this I have this scar— *(He pulls up his sleeve)* Will never go away. For this I am paid six cents an hour. Six. Unless one of the bottles breaks, then I am paid five. This is my job. This is the "someone who will have to make another one." Me! Now what you think?

GUITEAU: I think you should get another job.

CZOLGOSZ: What other job?! There is no other job!

GUITEAU: Don't be ridiculous. Why, look at me: I've been an attorney, an evangelist, I've sold insurance. I'm a celebrated author. Last week I was a bill collector, and next week I'm going to be Ambassador to France!

CZOLGOSZ: I can't be no "celebrated author." I can't be no Ambassador to France.

GUITEAU: Can't, can't, can't. You know your problem? You're a pessimist. This isn't Poland, old boy. This is America! The Land of Opportunity!

CZOLGOSZ: Opportunity for who?! *(Indicating Hinckley)* For him?! For you?! *(He seizes the bottle)* This is only opportunity for me! This! Only this!

(He raises the bottle as if to smash it on the bar. Everybody stares. He hesitates, the bottle held above his head)

BOOTH: Go on. Break it.

(Czolgosz doesn't move)

See how it feels . . . It'll feel good . . . Just try it. Break the bottle . . . *Break it.*

SCENE 4

*Through the radio we hear applause, then, as the bar and the
Assassins disappear, the filtered voice of an Announcer, under
which a band is playing the Sousa march, "El Capitan."*

ANNOUNCER'S VOICE: That was President-elect Franklin D.
Roosevelt, ladies and gentlemen, speaking to a crowd of
supporters here in Miami's beautiful Bayfront Park. A
group of notables are pressing in around the President-
elect's car. There's Mayor Anton Cermak of Chicago, and—

(BANG!—a gunshot. Screams and confusion. The band stops)

There's been a shot! I can't see—wait! Mr. Roosevelt is
waving! He's all right! But Mayor Cermak has been hit! The
police have somebody in custody. An immigrant. Giuseppe
Zangara. We take you now to a group of eyewitnesses who
will tell us what they saw!

*(Lights up on five Bystanders, clustered around a microphone, and
a Photographer off to one side. The band resumes "El Capitan,"
which continues underneath)*

BYSTANDER #1 (MAN) *(Suddenly coming to life and seizing the
microphone, sings)*:
We're crowded up close,
And I see this guy,
He's squeezing by,
I catch his eye,

29

I say to him, "Where do you
Think you're trying to go, boy?
Whoa, boy!"
I say, "Listen, you runt,
You're not pulling that stunt—
No gentleman pushes their way to the front."
I say, "Move to the back!", which he does with a grunt—
Which is how I saved Roosevelt!

BYSTANDER #2 (MAN) *(Pushing #1 away from the microphone)*:
Then—
Well, I'm in my seat,
I get up to clap,
I feel this tap,
I turn—this sap,
He says he can't see,
I say, "Find a lap
And go sit
On it!"
Which is how I saved—!

BYSTANDER #3 (WOMAN) *(Overlapping, interrupting hysterically)*:
Then—
He started to swear
And he climbed on a chair,
He was aiming a gun—I was standing right there—
So I pushed it as hard as I could in the air—!
Which is how I saved Roosevelt!

ALL THREE *(To the tune of "El Capitan")*:
Lucky I was there—

BYSTANDER #1:
That's why he was standing back too far—!

BYSTANDERS #2 AND #3:
>   That's why when he aimed, he missed the car—!

ALL THREE:
>   Just lucky I was there—!
>   Or we'd have been left
>   Bereft
>   Of FDR!

(Crashing chord, gloomy; sudden light on Zangara, strapped into the electric chair)

ZANGARA *(Front)*:
>   You think that I scare?
>   No scare.
>   You think that I care?
>   No care.
>   I look at the world—
>   No good. No fair. Nowhere.

(Tarantella music begins, cheerful)

>   When I am a boy,
>   No school.
>   I work in a ditch.
>   No chance.
>   The smart and the rich
>   Ride by,
>   Don't give no glance.

>   Ever since then, because of them,
>   I have the sickness in the stomach,
>   Which is the way I make my idea
>   To go out and kill Roosevelt.

(Bass drum: Photographer takes flash photo of Bystanders)

>   First I was figure I kill Hoover,
>   I get even for the stomach.
>   Only Hoover up in Washington,

31

ASSASSINS

Is wintertime in Washington,
Too cold for the stomach in Washington—
I go down to Miami, kill Roosevelt.

No laugh—!
No funny!
Men with the money,
They control everything.

Roosevelt, Hoover—
No make no difference.
You think I care who I kill?
I no care who I kill,
Long as it's king!

("El Capitan" becomes prominent again)

BYSTANDER #4 (MAN):
    The crowd's breaking up
    When I hear these shots,
    And I mean lots—

BYSTANDER #5 (HIS WIFE) *(Interrupting)*:
    I thought I'd plotz—

MAN:
    I spotted him—

WIFE *(Overlapping)*:
    My stomach was tied in knots—

MAN:
    So I barreled—

WIFE:
    Harold—!
    No, what happened was this:
    He was blowing a kiss—

MAN:

She means Roosevelt—

WIFE *(Going right on, overlapping)*:

I was saying to Harold, "This weather is bliss!"

MAN:

When you think that we might have missed seeing him
    miss—!

BOTH:

Lucky we were there!

WIFE:

It was a historical event—!

MAN:

—Worth every penny that we spent!

ALL FIVE BYSTANDERS:

Just lucky we were there—!

BYSTANDER #1 *(To the tune of "The Washington Post")*:

To think, if I'd let him get up closer—!

BYSTANDER #3:

I saw right away he was insane—

(Dragging a reluctant Bystander #2 forward)

Oh, this is my husband, we're from Maine—

BYSTANDER #2:

He told me to sit, but I said, "No, sir!"—

BYSTANDER #4:

It made our vacation a real success!

(Bass drum: flash)

BYSTANDER #5 *(Reacts; to Photographer)*:

Are you with the press?

PHOTOGRAPHER: Yes.

BYSTANDER #5:
Oh God, I'm a mess . . .

BYSTANDER #1:
Some left wing foreigner, that's my guess—

ZANGARA:
No!

BYSTANDERS:
And wasn't the band just fantastic?

ZANGARA *(Overlapping)*:
No—
—Left!

You think I am Left?
No Left, no Right,
No anything!
Only American!

Zangara have nothing,
No luck, no girl,
Zangara no smart, no school,
But Zangara no foreign tool,
Zangara American!
American nothing!

(Furious)

And why there no photographers?
For Zangara no photographers!
Only capitalists get photographers!
No right!

BYSTANDERS:
Lucky I was there!
I'm on the front page—is that bizarre?

34

And all of those pictures, like a star!
Just lucky I was there!
We might have been left bereft of F—

ZANGARA *(Simultaneously)*:
No fair
Nowhere!
So what?
No sorry!
And soon no Zangara!

Who care?
Pull switch!
No care
No more,
No—

(Electrical hum; the lights dim briefly, then rise)

BYSTANDERS:
—D—

(Hum; lights dim briefly and rise again)

R!

(Hum; lights dim briefly and go out)

SCENE 5

An anarchist rally in Chicago, summer 1901. Leon Czolgosz, surrounded by a sea of working men, listens raptly to the offstage speaker, Emma Goldman.

GOLDMAN'S VOICE: What does a man do when before his eyes he sees a vision of a new hope dawning for his toiling, agonizing brothers? What does a man do when at last he realizes that his suffering is caused not by the cruelty of fate, but by the injustice of his fellow human beings? What does a man do when he sees those dear to him starving, when he himself is starved? What does he do? What does he do? What—

(The piercing shriek of a police whistle. Shouts, curses, the sound of chairs being overturned. Czolgosz stands, transfixed, as the scene around him fades and changes to the sidewalk outside a Chicago row house; it is the following morning. The door to the row house opens and Emma Goldman comes out, carrying a suitcase. One of her arms is in a sling)

CZOLGOSZ: Miss Goldman?

GOLDMAN: I am Emma Goldman. Who are you?

CZOLGOSZ: My name is Czolgosz. Leon Czolgosz. I would like to speak with you—

GOLDMAN: I'm sorry, but I have a train to catch.

(She starts to leave)

CZOLGOSZ: *Miss Goldman—*

(She stops)

I was in the hall last night. I heard your speech. It was—very good.

GOLDMAN: Thank you. The cossacks of the Chicago Police Department seemed to feel otherwise.

CZOLGOSZ: They are the vilest scum in the world!

GOLDMAN: You haven't seen much of the world, have you, Mr. Czolgosz?

CZOLGOSZ: No. Yes. I have been to Buffalo, to Rochester, to Cleveland—

GOLDMAN: Yes? And when were you in Cleveland?

CZOLGOSZ: Last week.

GOLDMAN: And Rochester?

CZOLGOSZ: The week before.

GOLDMAN: And the week before you were in Buffalo.

(He nods)

You have been following me. Why? *(A beat)* Answer me! Why?! To spy on me?! To inform on my associates?! Who sent you?! Who—

CZOLGOSZ: Miss Goldman, I am in love with you!

GOLDMAN: What?

CZOLGOSZ: I am in love with you.

GOLDMAN *(A beat)*: Ah! That's different. Thank you, Mr. Czolgosz. Leon. Unfortunately I do not have time to be in love with you. I am speaking tonight in St. Louis and if I miss my train, the cossacks there will have to find somebody else's arm to break.

CZOLGOSZ: If I could, I would protect you! I would strike them down!

GOLDMAN: You can.

CZOLGOSZ: What?

GOLDMAN: Strike them down.

(He looks bewildered)

You don't understand. Not yet. Ah, well. You remind me how much work I have yet to do. Goodbye, Leon—

(She starts to go)

CZOLGOSZ: Miss Goldman! Wait!

(She turns)

Miss Goldman, I am alone, with no one and with nothing! I am a grown man, twenty-seven, but I have no life! What do I know?! Nothing! What have I learned?! Nothing! What have I done—!

GOLDMAN *(Interrupting)*: I'll tell you what you have done. Since you were a little boy of five or six you have permitted yourself to be brutalized and beaten down, brought to the brink of madness by despair and desperation, so that other men, men no worthier than you, might live their lives in ease and comfort. *This* is what you have done. This is what they have done to you . . . Am I right?

(She beckons to him)

Come, Leon. Come.

(He steps up to her. She kisses him)

You are a beautiful young man.

CZOLGOSZ: I am coarse and ugly.

GOLDMAN: No. Your life has made you beautiful. Your suffering has made you fine.

(She strokes his cheek)

I give my love freely, Leon. If I had time I would give it to you. But I don't. So instead I will give you something else. Something you can embrace with more passion than you can any woman.

(She takes a pamphlet from her pocket and hands it to him)

CZOLGOSZ: What is this?

GOLDMAN: An idea, Leon. An idea of social justice. Of a world in which men are not merely created equal but allowed to live that way.

CZOLGOSZ: And this is your idea?

GOLDMAN: Not mine alone, but mine.

(He puts the pamphlet in his pocket. She smiles, looks at her watch)

Good God! I have to go—

CZOLGOSZ: If you please—I would like to walk you to the station. May I?

GOLDMAN: It's a free country. *(A beat)* That was a joke.

CZOLGOSZ: May I?

GOLDMAN: You may.

(He takes her suitcase; she takes it back)

They make us servants, Leon. We do not make servants of each other.

(He looks at her, then takes the suitcase. She smiles. They exit)

SCENE 6

A public park. Squeaky Fromme is sitting by herself, smoking a joint. Sara Jane Moore enters, juggling her purse, a couple of cans of Tab, and a big bucket of Kentucky Fried Chicken. She starts to drop the purse; she grabs for it—BANG! *A gun goes off inside the purse.*

MOORE: Shit! I'm sorry. Could you give me a hand with this? *(She hands Fromme the chicken)* Thanks. I got the Extra Crispy, I hope that's O.K. And they were out of fries, so I got onion rings—

FROMME: I can't believe they even sell this stuff, man. It's so plastic.

MOORE: Plastic? Oh, *plastic.* Yeah, it's really plastic.

FROMME: So how come you buy it?

MOORE: Me? I don't. I mean, unless, you know, I'm stuck at the beauty parlor, and I haven't done the marketing, and it's time to pick Billy up at Little League—

(Moore opens a Tab and starts eating chicken)

FROMME: Charlie says that fast food is the stinking swill Americans lap up the way a dog returns to its own vomit. Charlie says that in America the chickens are finally coming home to roost, rotting and reeking with the oozing pus of a society devouring its own anus.

MOORE: Who's Charlie?

FROMME: Charlie Manson!

40

MOORE: Charlie Manson, *the mass murderer?* Is he a friend of yours?

FROMME: I'm his lover and his slave.

MOORE: Far out!

(Fromme takes a hit on the joint and passes it to Moore)

You know, it's really weird. I knew a guy named Charlie Manson back in high school. I also knew a guy named Guy Lombardo. God, what a dreamboat! He was captain of the football team—

(Moore takes a big drag on the joint)

FROMME: Charlie says that football is a form of slavery in which the black man's speed and strength are ruthlessly exploited by the racist ruling class. Charlie says that one day the black man will throw off his chains and lash back at the pigs who have tormented him. Charlie says that in the Armageddon which ensues, women will be raped and disemboweled. Men will be castrated, lynched and burned alive. Blood and gore will choke our streets. And after the two sides have wiped each other out, Charlie will emerge as king of a new order, with me beside him as his queen.

MOORE: I love your beads.

FROMME: My what?

MOORE: Your beads. I must've spent an hour on Haight Street trying to find a string of beads like that, but all I found were these. *(Indicates her own beads)* The salesman told me they were groovy, but I don't think they're groovy. I think *yours* are groovy. In fact, I think they're psychedelic.

(Fromme snickers)

What's so funny?

FROMME: "Groovy." "Psychedelic." The way you talk, you sound just like a narc.

MOORE: I am a narc.

FROMME: *What?*

MOORE: I mean I was. They fired me.

FROMME: Who fired you?

MOORE: The FBI.

FROMME: You worked for the *FBI*?

MOORE: Right before I was a CPA. No, wait. Right after. Who was my husband then? Jack? No, Jack was when I had amnesia.

FROMME: You had *amnesia*?

MOORE: You're kidding me? I *did*?

(Moore laughs, Fromme stares)

It's a joke! See, it's like if I had amnesia, then I couldn't remember anything, including that I had amnesia.

FROMME: Are you making this stuff up?

MOORE: I don't know. I mean, I'm not, but I don't know. Was I really in the Women's Army Corps? Have I really had five husbands? If I had three kids, where are they?

FROMME: I was like you once. Lost. Confused. A piece of shit.

(Moore nods philosophically)

Then I met Charlie . . . I was sitting on the beach in Venice. I'd just had a big fight with my daddy about, I don't know, my eye make-up or the bombing of Cambodia. He said I was a drug addict and a whore and I should get out of his house forever—

MOORE: I think there's a new perfume called Charlie.

FROMME: I went down to the beach and sat down on the sand and cried. I felt like I was disappearing. Like the whole world was dividing into two parts. Me, and everybody else. And then this guy came down the beach, this dirty-looking little elf. He stopped in front of me and smiled this twinkly devil smile and said, "Your daddy kicked you out." He knew! "Your daddy kicked you out!" How could he know? My daddy didn't tell him, so who could've? *God*. God sent this dirty-looking little elf to save a little girl lost on a beach. He smiled again and touched my hair and off he went. And for a minute I just watched him go. Then I ran and caught his hand, and till they arrested him for stabbing Sharon Tate, I never let it go.

(Moore starts to cry)

FROMME: What's wrong?

MOORE: He reminds me of *my* daddy.

FROMME: Who does?

(Moore indicates the chicken bucket; on it is a large portrait of Colonel Sanders)

Colonel Sanders?

MOORE: My daddy was like your daddy. I loved him so much, and he said that he loved me, and then he threw me out.

FROMME: Let's kill him.

MOORE: O.K. How?

(Fromme stares dagger eyes at the portrait of Colonel Sanders)

What are you doing?

FROMME: Giving him the evil eye.

MOORE: That's a picture on a box of chicken.

FROMME: It's a graven image. Charlie taught us how to do it.

MOORE: And you can really kill someone like that?

(Fromme nods)

Wow!

(They both stare at the picture on the bucket. A long beat)

MOORE: This is neat.

FROMME: Shhhh!

(They stare. Another beat)

MOORE: You think it's working?

FROMME: I don't know.

MOORE: Then let's try this—

(Moore whips out her gun and shoots the bucket—BANG!
Fromme squeals with glee and does the same. They empty their
guns, laughing and shrieking like schoolgirls. Then they collapse,
catching their breath)

FROMME: So. Where you from?
MOORE: West Virginia.

(Fromme screams)

What's the matter?!
FROMME: That's where Charlie's from!
MOORE: You're kidding. Where in West Virginia?
FROMME: Charleston.

(Moore screams)

What's the matter?!
MOORE: That's where *I'm* from!

(Fromme screams)

You don't suppose . . .
FROMME: My Charlie drives a Harley-Davidson he says he's had
   since high school—
MOORE: My Charlie smoked Kools with the filters bitten off—
FROMME: My Charlie has "Eat Shit and Die" tattooed on his
   chest—
MOORE: My Charlie and your Charlie are the same!

(They both scream)

FROMME: You knew him when he was just a kid!
MOORE: With skinny legs and acne and no chin!
FROMME: Could you tell he was the son of God?
MOORE *(A beat)*: *Absolutely.*

(Fromme screams. Moore screams. They keep on screaming. Their
screams rise, out of control, as the lights fade to black)

Scene Four. Five Bystanders in Bayfront Park, Miami, Florida, February 15, 1933.

Scene Three. John Hinckley (Greg Germann), The Bartender (John Jellison), Charles Guiteau (Jonathan Hadary) and Giuseppe Zangara (Eddie Korbich) at a turn of the century saloon. (Following page): Scene One. A Shooting Gallery.

Scene Four. Giuseppe Zangara (Eddie Korbich) strapped into the electric chair.

*Scene Five. Emma Goldman (Lyn Greene)
and Leon Czolgosz (Terrence Mann)
after an anarchist rally in Chicago,
summer 1901.*

*Scene Six. Lynette ("Squeaky")
Fromme (Annie Golden) and
Sara Jane Moore (Debra Monk)
in a public park.*

*(Right): Scene Twelve. Charles Guiteau
(Jonathan Hadary), The Hangman
(Marcus Olson) and The Balladeer
(Patrick Cassidy). (Below): Scene Fourteen.
Samuel Byck (Lee Wilkoff) behind
the wheel of a '67 Buick.*

*Scene Ten. John Hinckley (Greg Germann) and Lynette ("Squeaky") Fromme
(Annie Golden) in the basement rec room at Hinckley's parents' house.*

Scene Fifteen. "Another National Anthem."

Scene Sixteen. A storeroom on the sixth floor of the Texas School Book Depository in Dallas, Texas.

SCENE 7

Lights up on Czolgosz, alone, examining an empty pistol.

CZOLGOSZ *(Sings)*:
It takes a lot of men to make a gun,
Hundreds,
Many men to make a gun:

Men in the mines
To dig the iron,
Men in the mills
To forge the steel,
Men at machines
To turn the barrel,
Mold the trigger,
Shape the wheel—
It takes a lot of men to make a gun . . .
One gun . . .

(Booth appears)

BOOTH *(Softly)*:
And all you have to do
Is
Move your little finger,
Move your little finger and—

(Czolgosz clicks the trigger)

You can change the world.

Why should you be blue
When
You've your little finger?
Prove how just a little finger
Can—

(Czolgosz clicks the trigger again)

Change the world.

CZOLGOSZ *(Simultaneously)*:
I hate this gun . . .

(Guiteau waltzes in cheerfully, holding a gun up admiringly)

GUITEAU:
What a wonder is a gun!
What a versatile invention!
First of all, when you've a gun—

(He points it out front, slowly panning over the audience; music stops)

Everybody pays attention.

(Music resumes)

When you think what must be done,
Think of all that it can do:
Remove a scoundrel,
Unite a party,
Preserve the Union,
Promote the sales of my book—
Insure my future,
My niche in history,
And then the world will see
That I am not a man to overlook!
Ha-ha!

GUITEAU, BOOTH & CZOLGOSZ:
And all you have to do
Is
Squeeze your little finger.
Ease your little finger back—

(They click the triggers)

You can change the world.
Whatever else is true,
You
Trust your little finger.
Just a single little finger
Can—

(They click again)

Change the world.

(Sara Jane Moore enters, fishing through her large purse)

MOORE:
I got this really great gun—

(Fishing)

Shit, where is it?
No, it's really great—
Wait—

(Pulls out a lipstick, drops it back)

Shit, where is it?
Anyway—

(Continuing to fish)

It's just a .38—

(Pulls out a large hairbrush)

But—

(Drops it back, keeps fishing)

It's a gun,
And you can make a state—
—ment—

(Pulls out a shoe)

Wrong—

With a gun—
Even if you fail.
It tells 'em who you are,
Where you stand.
This one was on sale. It—
No, not the shoe—
Well, actually the shoe was, too.

(Drops it back in, fishes around)

No, that's not it—
Shit, I had it here—
Got it!

(Pulls gun out, waves it around)

Yeah! There it is! And—

ALL FOUR *(Barbershop style)*:
   All you have to do
   Is
   Crook your little finger,
   Hook your little finger 'round—

(They pull their triggers; the men's guns click; Moore's goes off—
BLAM!*)*

MOORE:
   Shit, I shot it . . .

OTHERS:
   —You can change the world.

QUARTET:
> Simply follow through,
> And look, your little finger
> Can
> Slow them down
> To a crawl,
> Show them all,
> Big and small,
> It
> Took a little finger
> No time
> To change the world.

(All exit, except Czolgosz, who continues to examine his gun)

CZOLGOSZ:
> A gun kills many men before it's done,
> Hundreds,
> Long before you shoot the gun:
>
> Men in the mines
> And in the steel mills,
> Men at machines,
> Who died for what?
>
> Something to buy—
> A watch, a shoe, a gun,
> A "thing" to make the bosses richer,
> But
> A gun claims many men before it's done . . .
>
> Just one . . .
> More . . .

(Czolgosz puts the gun in his pocket as, behind him, lights come up on . . .)

SCENE 8

The Temple of Music Pavilion at the Pan-American Exposition in Buffalo, New York. It is September 6, 1901. The Balladeer enters.

BALLADEER *(Sings)*:
Czolgosz,
Working man,
Born in the middle of Michigan,
Woke with a thought
And away he ran
To the Pan-American Exposition
In Buffalo,
In Buffalo.

Saw of a sudden
How things were run,
Said, "Time's a-wasting,
It's nineteen-one.
Some men have everything
And some have none,
So rise and shine—
In the U.S.A.
You can work your way
To the head of the line!"

(Lights come up on half a dozen Fairgoers, including a Little Boy with a bottle of soda. They are the epitome of bourgeois prosperity and complacency. They are standing on a receiving line, waiting to

shake hands with President William McKinley. The receiving line is defined by potted palms and American flags and is supervised by a uniformed Attendant)

ATTENDANT: Single line, ladies and gentlemen. Line forms here to meet the President of the United States. Single line to shake hands with President William McKinley—

BALLADEER:
Czolgosz,
Quiet man,
Worked out a quiet
And simple plan,
Strolled of a morning,
All spick and span,
To the Temple of Music
By the Tower of Light
At the Pan-American Exposition
In Buffalo,
In Buffalo.

(Czolgosz begins to make his way to the end of the line)

Saw Bill McKinley there,
In the sun.
Heard Bill McKinley say,
"Folks, have fun!
Some men have everything
And some have none,
But that's just fine:
In the U.S.A.
You can work your way
To the head of the line!"

FAIRGOERS *(Looking at McKinley)*:
Big Bill—!

BALLADEER:
>—Gave 'em a thrill.

FAIRGOERS:
>Big Bill—!

BALLADEER:
>—Sold 'em a bill.

FAIRGOERS:
>Big Bill!

BALLADEER:
>Who'd want to kill
>A man of good will
>Like—?

FAIRGOERS, BALLADEER:
>Big Bill!

(Note: The following three speeches should be slightly stylized)

FAIRGOER #1: Doesn't the President look marvelous? So round and prosperous!

FAIRGOER #2: Do you know what his favorite dish is? It was in the papers. *Beef.*

FAIRGOER #3: I'm told that in his spare time he enjoys collecting coins!

(Czolgosz reaches the end of the line; he takes out a handkerchief and mops his brow. The Little Boy holds out his soda bottle)

LITTLE BOY: Want a sip?

(Czolgosz takes the bottle, looks at it)

CZOLGOSZ: No, thank you.

(He hands the bottle back, takes out his gun and wraps it in the handkerchief)

BALLADEER:
>Czolgosz,
>Angry man,

Said, "I will do what
A poor man can.
Yes, and there's nowhere
More fitting than
In the Temple of Music
By the Tower of Light
Between the Fountain of Abundance
And the Court of Lilies
At the great Pan-American Exposition
In Buffalo,
In Buffalo."

Wrapped him a handkerchief
'Round his gun,
Said, "Nothin' wrong about
What I done.
Some men have everything,
And some have none—
That's by design.
The idea wasn't mine alone,
But mine—
And that's the sign:

In the U.S.A.
You can have your say,
You can set your goals
And seize the day,
You've been given the freedom
To work your way
To the head of the line—

(Czolgosz at last reaches McKinley—and shoots—BANG!)

To the head of the line!"

(Blackout)

SCENE 9

A park bench. Sam Byck trudges on, wearing his Santa Claus suit, carrying his picket sign and a beat-up shopping bag. He sits down, reaches in the shopping bag, takes out a can of Yoo-Hoo, opens it, and takes a big drink. He then takes out a greasy sandwich, a portable tape recorder and a bunch of tapes. He shoves a tape in the tape recorder, takes a bite of sandwich, composes himself and starts recording.

BYCK: Hello, Mr. Bernstein? Lenny? How you doin'? My name is Sam Byck. We've never met. You're a world-renowned composer and conductor who travels the world over enjoying one success after another and I'm an out-of-work tire salesman, so I guess that's not surprising. But I hope you'll take a few minutes out of your busy schedule to listen to this tape which you just opened in the mail. If you can't listen to it now, maybe you can listen to it— *(He sings)*

Tonight, tonight . . .

(He chuckles cheerfully) I love that song. What a melody! And what a sentiment. "Tonight, tonight, I'll meet my love tonight . . ." Where is she, Lenny? Gimme a hint. *(He takes a drink of Yoo-Hoo and a big bite of the sandwich)* Lenny, you're a modest kind of guy, I know that. But you'll indulge me for a minute if I say something from the heart. You're a genius. Yes, you are! And you know why? You understand what

people want. You have their ear. You make 'em listen, Lenny. No one listens. Are you listening?! No one listens . . . *(He takes another bite of sandwich)* Well, if you're hearing this, I guess you're listening now, right? So with all due respect, deferring to your stature in the world of music, classical and semi-classical, I want to offer you a small piece of advice . . . Hey, I know what you're thinking. Who the hell is Sam Byck with his fat ass and his tongue on rye to give a shit hot guy such as yourself advice? Well, Lenny, it's a fact that my unwillingness to compromise my principles and kiss ass like some people I could mention has cost me the so-called good life which others have enjoyed. So be it, Len. Fuck me, fuck you. But Lenny, listen. Listen to one small piece of advice from a true fan . . . Forget the long-hair shit and write what you write best. *Love songs.* They're what we need! They're what the world needs! "Lonely Town!" "Maria!" Tender melodies to cherish for a lifetime! Timeless strains which linger in the memory and the heart! Love, Lenny! What the world needs now is love sweet love! Love makes the world go round! *(He takes a slurp of Yoo-Hoo)* Well, not exactly. Bullshit makes the world go round. You know that all too well, a worldly guy such as yourself. You know the world's a vicious, stinking pit of emptiness and pain. But not for long. I'm gonna change things, Lenny. I'm gonna drop a 747 on the White House and incinerate Dick Nixon. It's gonna make the news. You're gonna hear about it and I know what you're gonna ask yourself: What kind of world is this where a decent, stand-up guy like Sam Byck has to crash a plane into the President to make a point? You're gonna wonder if you want to go on living in a world like that. Well, lemme tell you, Len. You do. And you know why? So you can keep on writing love songs! Yes! There's a gorgeous world out there, a world of unicorns and waterfalls and puppy dogs! And you can save it! Through the medium of your God-given talent! *Do it*, Lenny! Save the world! Is that too much to ask?! . . . Oh, Lenny. One more thing. When you hear about my death you're gonna wonder if there's something more you could've done. Lenny, you did everything you could . . . *(He clicks off the tape recorder. A beat. Then he clicks it on again)* Well, maybe not *everything*. Maybe not absolutely everything, you know? Maybe one day you could've picked a phone up. Just picked up a phone and said, "Hey, Sammy, how's it going? Hang in there, Sam. This Bud's for you." How long would that have taken you? A minute? Half a minute? That was too much, wasn't it? You probably had your limo double parked. You and your shit hot buddies had a plane to catch to Paris, France for dinner and a blow job. Hey, I understand. I understand too well, my friend. You're just like all the rest of them— *(He flips through the tapes, reading names)* Jonas Salk, Jack Anderson, Hank Aaron . . . You knew where I was. You *all* did. And you know what you did? You left me there! You jerks! You shits! You pricks! You had your chance and now it's too damn late! Fuck me?! Fuck you! I'm outta here! I'm history, Lenny! Understand?! I'm *history*! *(He takes a big bite of his sandwich, chews. Lights fade, as he starts to sing . . .)*

I like to be in America,
O.K. by me in America,
Knobs on the doors in America,
Wall-to-wall floors in America!

(Blackout)

SCENE 10

Lights up on John Hinckley. He is sitting on the couch in the basement rec room at his parents' house, picking out a song on his guitar. An 8x10 photograph is propped up in front of him. Squeaky Fromme enters. Hinckley doesn't see her. She listens for a moment.

FROMME: You play the guitar?

HINCKLEY *(Startled)*: What? No.

FROMME: You're playing it.

HINCKLEY: I play a little. Just for myself.

FROMME: Can you play "Sympathy for the Devil?"

HINCKLEY: No.

FROMME: How 'bout "Helter Skelter?"

HINCKLEY: No.

FROMME: What *can* you play?

HINCKLEY: I write my own songs.

FROMME: Yeah? Lemme hear one.

HINCKLEY: I told you. I just play for myself.

FROMME: Pretend I'm not here.

HINCKLEY *(His voice rising)*: Would you leave me alone? *Please?*

FROMME *(Picking up the photograph)*: Who's this? Your girlfriend?

HINCKLEY *(Lunging for it)*: Gimme that!

FROMME: How old is she?

HINCKLEY: She's young, all right?!

FROMME: She looks like a whore.

HINCKLEY: She is a whore! So what?! I'm gonna save her from all that!

FROMME: You're full of it.

HINCKLEY: Yeah? Read what it says!

FROMME *(Reading the inscription on the picture)*: "Dear John. I will love you forever. One day you will come for me and we will occupy the White House and the peasants will drool with envy."

HINCKLEY: See!

FROMME: "This photograph the property of Universal Pictures. Any reproduction—"

HINCKLEY *(Snatching the picture back)*: *Gimme that!*

FROMME: That's a picture of a movie star.

HINCKLEY: So?

FROMME: You don't know any movie star. You wrote that yourself.

HINCKLEY: What if I did?! I've been to her dorm! I call her up! I've seen her movie sixteen times!

(Fromme takes out a tattered newspaper clipping)

FROMME: See this guy? I'm his girlfriend. I kiss him. I fuck him. I do stuff for him you wouldn't even understand. Does she do that for you? Does she kiss you? And fuck you? And—

HINCKLEY: Get out of here!

FROMME: You don't have a girlfriend!

HINCKLEY: *Get out!*

FROMME: Fruit . . .

(Fromme exits. A long beat. To photograph:)

HINCKLEY: My dearest Jodie. I am humiliated, by my weakness and my impotence. But, Jodie, I can change. I'll prove to you that I can change. With one brave, historic act I will win your love, now and for all eternity. Love, John.

(Hinckley picks up his guitar, steps downstage. He accompanies himself as he sings)

I am nothing,
You are wind and water and sky,
Jodie.
Tell me, Jodie, how I
Can earn your love.

I would swim oceans,
I would move mountains,
I would do anything for you.
What do you want me to do?

I am unworthy of your love,
Jodie, Jodie,
Let me prove worthy of your love.
Tell me how I can earn your love,
Set me free.
How can I turn your love
To me?

(He continues strumming; lights up on Squeaky Fromme on the other side of the stage, in limbo; she sings to Hinckley's accompaniment, but without acknowledging him)

FROMME:
I am nothing,
You are wind and devil and god,
Charlie,
Take my blood and my body
For your love.

Let me feel fire,
Let me drink poison,
Tell me to tear my heart in two,
If that's what you want me to do . . .

I am unworthy of your love,
Charlie, darlin',
I have done nothing for your love.

59

Let me be worthy of your love,
Set you free—

HINCKLEY:
I would come take you from your life . . .

FROMME:
I would come take you from your cell . . .

HINCKLEY:
You would be queen to me, not wife . . .

FROMME:
I would crawl belly-deep through hell . . .

HINCKLEY:
Baby, I'd die for you . . .

FROMME:
Baby, I'd die for you . . .

HINCKLEY:
Even though—

FROMME:
Even though—

HINCKLEY:	FROMME:
I will always know:	I will always know:
I am unworthy of your love,	I am unworthy of your love,
Jodie darlin',	Charlie darlin',

BOTH:
Let me prove worthy of your love.
I'll find a way to earn your love,
Wait and see.
Then you will turn your love to me,
Your love to me . . .

(A smiling, formally posed photograph of Ronald Reagan is projected upstage behind Hinckley. As Fromme watches, Hinckley

draws his gun, turns and shoots—BANG*! The picture disappears. Hinckley turns quietly downstage)*

HINCKLEY: He died so that our love could live.

(The photograph of Reagan reappears; Fromme smiles)

FROMME: Sorry, Nancy. Looks like I forgot to duck!

(Hinckley wheels and fires again. BANG*! The photograph of Reagan disappears, then reappears, brighter than before)*

I sure hope the surgeon's a Republican!

(Hinckley fires again. Reagan disappears, then reappears, brighter still)

Where'd this kid learn to shoot? The Russian Army?

(Hinckley fires frantically. Reagan disappears, then reappears)

There you go again—!

(Hinckley fires continuously, desperately. Reagan disappears and reappears, each time glowing brighter than before)

There you go again! There you go again! There you go again! . . .

(Lights fade to black)

SCENE 11

Lights up on Sara Jane Moore, taking target practice. She stands pigeon-toed, eyes closed, holding her gun with two hands, aiming it in the general direction of the Kentucky Fried Chicken bucket. She jerks the trigger—BANG! The bucket doesn't move.

MOORE: Shit.

(She walks up to the bucket, aims the gun directly at it—the barrel touches it—then starts slowly backing up. Charles Guiteau enters behind her. He stops and watches her. She stops in front of him, still aiming at the bucket. He puts his hands over her eyes)

GUITEAU: Guess who?

(Moore screams and spins around, firing wildly half a dozen times. Guiteau grins)

Did I surprise you?

MOORE: You scared me half to death!

GUITEAU: I am a terrifying and imposing figure! *(He chuckles happily)* You have been shooting at your lunch.

MOORE: I'm practicing.

GUITEAU: Practice makes perfect! Has your aim improved?

MOORE: I couldn't hit William Howard Taft if he were sitting on my lap.

GUITEAU: Show me your form.

MOORE: My what?

GUITEAU: The way you shoot.

MOORE: Oh, O.K. . . .

(Moore assumes her shooting stance—knock-kneed, eyes closed. Guiteau circles her, eyeing her appraisingly, particularly her bottom. He tries to look down her dress)

What do you think?

GUITEAU: The problem is your feet. To shoot well you must plant your feet and hold the gun out with a straight, stiff arm. Here, let me show you. *(He steps up behind her and puts his hands on her hips)* First the feet— *(He repositions her hips)* Then the arm. *(He puts his arms around her and holds her gun hand straight out)*

MOORE: Like this?

GUITEAU: You know, you are a very handsome woman.

MOORE: Thank you.

GUITEAU: How would you like to be the wife of the Ambassador to France?

MOORE: That would be nice.

GUITEAU *(Folding his arms around her)*: Come, let me steal a kiss.

MOORE: I don't think so.

GUITEAU: One little kiss.

MOORE: *Stop.*

GUITEAU: Ah! A coquette, eh?!

MOORE: Let go of me!

GUITEAU: *I want a kiss!*

(They struggle. Moore's gun goes off—BANG! Guiteau squeals and jumps back, holding his ear)

MOORE: Are you all right?

GUITEAU: I am more than all right! I am extraordinary! I am to be reckoned with! I am the next Ambassador to France!

(We hear the sound of trains. Moore exits. We are in the Baltimore & Potomac Railroad Station in Washington, July 2, 1881. President James Garfield enters, strolling arm in arm with his Secretary of State, James Blaine)

BLAINE: Your train is on Track 6, Mr. President.

GUITEAU: President Garfield!

GARFIELD: Yes?

GUITEAU: I want to be Ambassador to France!

GARFIELD: I'm sorry?

GUITEAU: *I want to be Ambassador to France!*

BLAINE *(To Garfield)*: Mad as a hatter.

> *(The two men chuckle and start to exit. Guiteau draws his gun, and shoots Garfield in the back —BANG! Garfield and Blaine freeze, their positions reflecting the positions of Garfield and Blaine in a nineteenth-century engraving of the assassination which is projected behind them. Lights fade on everything but Guiteau . . .)*

SCENE 12

Guiteau alone. As he sings, lights come up to reveal him at the foot of the gallows, the Hangman waiting at the top.

GUITEAU *(Unaccompanied)*:
I am going to the Lordy,
I am so glad.
I am going to the Lordy,
I am so glad.
I am going to the Lordy,
Glory hallelujah!
Glory hallelujah!
I am going to the Lordy . . .

(The Balladeer enters. He accompanies himself on banjo or guitar)

BALLADEER:
Come all ye Christians,
And learn from a sinner:
Charlie Guiteau.
Bound and determined
He'd wind up a winner,
Charlie had dreams
That he wouldn't let go.
Said, "Nothing to it,
I want it, I'll do it,
I'm Charles J. Guiteau."

Charlie Guiteau
Never said "never"
Or heard the word "no."
Faced with disaster,
His heart would beat faster,
His smile would just grow,
And he'd say:

GUITEAU *(Cakewalking cheerfully up and down the gallows steps):*
Look on the bright side,
Look on the bright side,
Sit on the right side
Of the Lord.
This is the land of
Opportunity,
He is your lightning,
You His sword.

Wait till you see tomorrow,
Tomorrow you get your reward!
You can be sad
Or you can be President—
Look on the bright side . . .

(Finishes a step or two higher than before)

I am going to the Lordy . . .

BALLADEER:
Charlie Guiteau
Drew a crowd to his trial,
Led them in prayer,
Said, "I killed Garfield,
I'll make no denial.
I was just acting
For Someone up there.

The Lord's my employer,
And now He's my lawyer,
So do what you dare."

Charlie said, "Hell,
If I am guilty,
Then God is as well."
But God was acquitted
And Charlie committed
Until he should hang.
Still, he sang:

GUITEAU *(Faster and shriller, cakewalking up and down the steps)*:
Look on the bright side,
Not on the black side.
Get off your backside,
Shine those shoes!
This is your golden
Opportunity:
You are the lightning
And you're news!

Wait till you see tomorrow,
Tomorrow you won't be ignored!
You could be pardoned,
You could be President—
Look on the bright side . . .

(Finishes a step or two higher)

I am going to the Lordy . . .

BALLADEER:
Charlie Guiteau
Had a crowd at the scaffold—

GUITEAU:
I am so glad . . .

BALLADEER:
> —Filled up the square,
> So many people
> That tickets were raffled.
> Shine on his shoes,
> Charlie mounted the stair,
> Said, "Never sorrow,
> Just wait till tomorrow,
> Today isn't fair.
> Don't despair . . ."

GUITEAU *(Feverishly, cakewalking up the steps)*:
> Look on the bright side,
> Look on the bright side,
> Sit on the right side . . .

> *(Reaches the Hangman, hesitates)*

> Of the . . .

> *(Steps backwards to the bottom, hesitates again, then with resolution cakewalks slowly back up, gathering momentum)*

> I am going to the Lordy,
> I am so glad!
> I am going to the Lordy,
> I am so glad!
> I have unified my party,
> I have saved my country.
> I shall be remembered!

> I am going to the Lordy . . .

> *(Hangman adjusts noose)*

BALLADEER:
> Look on the bright side,
> Not on the sad side,

Inside the bad side
Something's good!
This is your golden
Opportunity:
You've been a preacher—

GUITEAU:

Yes, I have!

BALLADEER:

You've been an author—

GUITEAU:

Yes, I have!

BALLADEER:

You've been a killer—

GUITEAU:

Yes, I have!

BALLADEER:

You could be an angel—

GUITEAU:

Yes, I could!

(Hangman puts hood over Guiteau)

BALLADEER:

Just wait until tomorrow,
Tomorrow they'll all climb aboard!
What if you never
Got to be President?
You'll be remembered—

(Guiteau dances briefly)

Look on the bright side—

(Again)

Trust in tomorrow—

(Once more)

GUITEAU, BALLADEER:
And the Lord!

(As the Hangman pulls the trap door lever, blackout)

SCENE 13

Darkness. A gunshot, and a yelp. Lights up on Sara Jane Moore. She is standing, gun in hand, her purse over her arm, staring down at the inert form of a small dog which lies at her feet.

MOORE: Shit!

(Squeaky Fromme enters, looking nervously around)

FROMME: Everything all set?

MOORE: Yeah. Everything is great.

FROMME: What's wrong?

MOORE: I just shot my dog.

FROMME: Your *dog*? You brought your *dog* to an assassination?

MOORE: What was I supposed to do with him, leave him in the car?

FROMME: You could've left him home!

MOORE: And come back to find the couch all chewed up? No, thanks!

FROMME: I don't *believe* this! How could you do something so *dumb*! How could you—

MOORE *(Picking up the dog)*: He's dead, all right? Let's drop it.

(She shoves the dead dog in her purse. A nine-year-old Boy enters)

BOY: Mom! Hey, mom! I need another fifty cents!

FROMME: You brought your *kid*?

MOORE: School was closed, I forgot to check the schedule, *all right*?

FROMME: This is *incredible!*
BOY: *Mom*—
MOORE: What is it?
BOY: I need another fifty cents.
MOORE: I gave you a dollar.
BOY: It's a dollar fifty.
MOORE: For an *ice cream?*
BOY: It's not an *ice cream.* It's a Bubbalo Bill. The eyes are made of
    M & M's and the nose is made of bubble gum!
MOORE: A dollar fifty is too much for an ice cream.
BOY: It's not an ice cream!
MOORE: You'll have to get something else.
BOY: I don't *want* something else!
MOORE: I'm sorry.
BOY: *You promised!*
MOORE: I did *not* promise.
BOY: Yes, you did!
MOORE: I did *not!* And I am not giving you another fifty cents for
    a *Bubbalo Bill. Period!*

(The Boy begins to wail)

FROMME: Jesus Christ.
MOORE: Just ignore him.

(The Boy wails louder)

Billy, stop it.

(He keeps wailing)

I said *stop* it.

(He wails louder)

Billy—

*(Moore draws her gun and points it at the Boy's head. Fromme
takes some change out of her pocket and shoves it at the Boy)*

FROMME: Here!

(He takes it, sticks his tongue out at Moore and runs off)

Your kid's an asshole.

MOORE: He has a learning disability.

FROMME: He's an asshole.

MOORE: *You're* an asshole.

FROMME: You're a *stupid* asshole.

MOORE: Teenage slut!

FROMME: Stupid housewife!

MOORE: I'd rather be a stupid housewife than a teenage slut! Sitting in a stupid mall someplace, listening to some stupid music with a bunch of stupid girlfriends. Nothing to do, nowhere to go. No wonder you wound up with a creep like Charlie Manson.

FROMME: *Me?* How 'bout you, with your *five husbands?* At least Charlie is the Son of God.

MOORE: Charlie's an asshole.

FROMME: Take that back.

MOORE: No.

FROMME: *Yes.*

MOORE: *No!*

FROMME: *Yes!*

(Fromme draws her gun and trains it on Moore. Moore draws her gun and trains it on Fromme. A long beat)

MOORE: This is ridiculous. Look, we came here to kill the President. Let's just kill him and go home, O.K.?

FROMME *(A beat; grudgingly)*: O.K.

(They lower their weapons)

Did you check your gun?

MOORE: Of course I checked my gun.

FROMME: It's loaded?

MOORE: Of course it's loaded.

FROMME: Are you sure?

MOORE: It wouldn't be much use if it wasn't loaded, would it?

(She waves the gun. The cylinder falls open and all the bullets fall out)

Shit!

(Fromme rolls her eyes. They drop to their knees and start picking up the bullets. Gerald Ford strolls on. He stumbles, regains his balance, watches for a minute)

FORD: Need some help?

MOORE: What? No, that's O.K.—

FORD: My pleasure!

(Ford gets down on his knees and starts helping them collect the bullets)

FORD: Say, you should be more careful with these things. They're *bullets*.

(The dead dog falls out of Moore's purse. Ford pets it)

Good doggie!

(Moore shoves the dog back in the purse)

FROMME: I think that's all of them.

FORD: Hang on. There's something in my ear.

(Ford reaches behind his ear, produces a bullet, grins and hands it to Moore)

MOORE: Thanks, Mr.—

FORD: Ford. Gerry Ford.

MOORE: *President* Gerry Ford?

FORD *(A beat)*: Yeah!

(Ford smiles and starts to exit. Fromme aims her gun at his back and pulls the trigger—CLICK)

FROMME: It didn't go off!

(Moore looks frantically at the bullets she holds in one hand and the gun she holds in the other. Then she starts to throw the bullets, one by one, at the departing President)

MOORE: Bang . . . Bang! . . . *Shit!*

(Blackout)

SCENE 14

Lights up on Sam Byck, behind the wheel of a '67 Buick, driving down a highway late at night. He looks bleary-eyed and strung out. The jacket of his Santa suit is unbuttoned, revealing a dirty T-shirt and a greasy set of suspenders. On the seat beside him are his tape recorder, a jumble of tapes, his Santa Claus beard, a copy of the Baltimore Sun, *a couple of cans of Budweiser and a paper bag from Burger King. He reaches into the Burger King bag, pulls out a hamburger and takes a bite . . .*

BYCK: "Have It Your Way." You know what my way is? *Hot.* How 'bout a hamburger that's fucking hot?! *(He hurls the hamburger out the window. A car horn blares)* Don't blame me! I'm from Massachusetts! *(He laughs, digs in the bag, pulls out a fistful of French fries, and talks into the tape recorder)* Dick, you still there, babe? Sorry about that. Ten miles from the airport, I'm starting to lose it here. Stay with me, baby. Talk me down—! *(He shoves the French fries in his mouth and takes a long drink of beer)* You know, Dick, in this, the waning hours of your administration, it seems appropriate to look back at your long years of public service and to conclude that, as our President, you really bit the big one. Wazoo city, babe. What can I say? And you know what? This cracks me up. I voted for you! Yes! I gave you my vote, my sacred democratic trust, and you know what you did? You pissed all over it! . . . Well, what the hell. Guys like you, you piss all over everything. You piss all over the country. You piss all over your-selves. You piss all over me . . . Yeah, yeah, I know. "Sam, don't say it! You're my main man! Guys like you, you're the backbone of the nation! Sammy—" *(Exploding) Shut up, Dick! I'm* talking now, all right?! I'm talking and *you're* listening! Here— *(He slaps the newspaper)* You seen a paper lately?! "Grandma Lives In Packing Crate!" "Sewage Closes Jersey Beaches!" "Saudi Prince Buys Howard Johnson's!" What the hell is going on here, Dick?! It wasn't supposed to be like this. It wasn't, but it *is.* And schmucks like you, you're telling us it *isn't!* Everything is fine! It's great! It's *Miller Time! What* Miller Time?! The woods are burn-ing, Dick! What can we do?! We want to make things *better! How*?! Let's hold an election! *Great.* The Democrat says he'll fix everything, the Republicans fucked up. The Republican says he'll fix everything, the Democrats fucked up. Who's telling us the truth? Who's lying? *Someone's* lying. *Who?* We read, we guess, we argue, but deep down we know that we don't know. How can we? Oil embargoes, megatons, holes in the ozone. Who can understand this crap? We need to believe, to trust like little kids, that someone wants what's best for us, that someone's looking out for us. That someone loves us. Do they? *No.* They lie to us! They lie about what's right, they lie about what's wrong, they lie about the fuckin' hamburgers! And when we realize they're lying, really real-ize it in our gut, then we get scared. Then we get terrified. Like children waking in the dark, we don't know where we are. "I had a bad dream! Mommy! Daddy! Sammy had a nightmare!" And daddy comes and takes me in his arms and says, "It's O.K., Sammy. Daddy's here. I love you, kid. Your mommy doesn't, but I do." And mommy comes and holds me tight and says, "I've got you, Bubala. I'm here for you. Your daddy isn't, but I am." . . . And then where are we? Who do we believe? What do we do?! *(A beat)* We do what we have to do. We kill the President.

(Grimly, Byck throws his hands in the air in a parody of Nixon's "V for Victory" sign. Car horns blare as lights fade and a collage of headlines is projected upstage, reporting Byck's assassination attempt, along with those of the other Assassins . . .)

SCENE 15

Crowd noises, blending into a slow, wordless lamentation, which continues quietly underneath; lights up on Czolgosz.

CZOLGOSZ: I did it because it is wrong for one man to have so much service when other men have none . . .

(Lights up on Booth)

BOOTH: I did it to bring down the government of Abraham Lincoln and to avenge the ravaged South . . .

(Orchestral music begins under the lamentation; lights up on Hinckley)

HINCKLEY: I did it to prove to her my everlasting love . . .

(Lights up on Fromme)

FROMME: I did it to make them listen to Charlie . . .

(Lights up on Zangara)

ZANGARA: I did it 'cause my belly was on fire . . .

(Lights up on Guiteau)

GUITEAU: I did it to preserve the Union and promote the sale of my book . . .

(Lights up on Moore)

MOORE: I did it so my friends would know where I was coming from . . .

BYCK *(Sings, muttering)*:
Where's my prize? . . .

(Lamentation stops; orchestral music continues under)

CZOLGOSZ: I did it because no one cared about the poor man's
pain . . .
MOORE: I did it so *I'd* know where I was coming from . . .

BYCK:
I want my prize . . .

ZANGARA: I did it 'cause the bosses made my belly burn . . .
HINCKLEY *(Overlapping)*: I did it so she'd pay attention . . .
MOORE *(Overlapping)*: So I'd have someplace to come from, and
someplace to go . . .
BYCK:
Don't I get a prize? . . .

GUITEAU: I did it because they said I'd be Ambassador to
France . . .
BOOTH: I did it so they'd suffer in the North the way we'd
suffered in the South . . .

BYCK *(Overlapping)*:
I deserve a fucking prize! . . .

FROMME: I did it so there'd be a trial, and Charlie would get to be
a witness, and he'd be on TV, and he'd save the world! . . .

GUITEAU:
Where's my prize? . . .

BYCK: I did it to make people *listen.*

CZOLGOSZ, FROMME:
They promised me a prize . . .

HINCKLEY: Because she wouldn't take my phone calls—

ALL *(Except Zangara)*:
>What about my prize? . . .

ZANGARA: Because nothing stopped the fire—!

ALL *(Except Byck)*:
>I want my prize! . . .

BYCK: *Nobody* would *listen!*

>*(Balladeer enters with guitar, sings to the Assassins, in wistful folk-style)*

BALLADEER:
>And it didn't mean a nickel,
>You just shed a little blood,
>And a lot of people shed a lot of tears.
>Yes, you made a little moment
>And you stirred a little mud—
>
>But it didn't fix the stomach
>And you've drunk your final Bud,
>And it didn't help the workers
>And it didn't heal the country
>And it didn't make them listen
>And they never said, "We're sorry"—

BYCK *(Mutters)*:
>Yeah, it's never gonna happen,
>Is it?
>No, sir—

CZOLGOSZ:
>Never.

BYCK:
>No, we're never gonna get the prize—

FROMME:
>No one listens . . .

ASSASSINS

BYCK:
—Are we?

ZANGARA:
Never.

BYCK:
No, it
Doesn't make a bit of difference,
Does it?

OTHERS *(Variously)*:
Didn't.
Ever.

BYCK:
Fuck it!

OTHERS:
Spread the word . . .

ALL:
Where's my prize? . . .

BALLADEER:
I just heard
On the news
Where the mailman won the lottery.
Goes to show:
When you lose, what you do is try again.

You can choose
What to be,
From a mailman to a President.
There are prizes all around you,
If you're wise enough to see:
The delivery boy's on Wall Street,
And the usherette's a rock star—

BYCK:

Right, it's never gonna happen, is it?

(Pause)

Is it!

HINCKLEY, FROMME:

No, man!

BYCK, CZOLGOSZ:

No, we'll never see the day arrive—

GROUP I:

Spread the word . . .

BYCK, CZOLGOSZ:

—Will we?

GROUP II:

No, sir—

ALL:

Never!

BYCK, CZOLGOSZ:

No one's ever gonna even care if we're alive,
Are they? . . .

GROUP I:

Never . . .

GROUP II:

Spread the word . . .

BYCK, CZOLGOSZ:

We're alive . . .

GROUP I:

Someone's gonna listen . . .

83

ALL:
> Listen!

BYCK *(Listening, quietly, front)*:
> Listen . . .
> There's another national anthem playing,
> Not the one you cheer
> At the ball park.

OTHERS:
> Where's my prize? . . .

BYCK:
> It's the other national anthem, saying—
> If you want to hear—
> It says, "Bullshit!" . . .

CZOLGOSZ:
> It says, "Never!"—

GUITEAU:
> It says, "Sorry!"—

GROUP II:
> Loud and clear—

ASSASSINS:
> It says: Listen
> To the tune that keeps sounding
> In the distance, on the outside,
> Coming through the ground,
> To the hearts that go on pounding
> To the sound
> Getting louder every year—!
>
> Listen to the sound . . .
> Take a look around . . .

We're
The other national anthem, folks,
The ones that can't get in
To the ball park.

Spread the word . . .

There's another national anthem, folks,
For those who never win,
For the suckers, for the pikers,
For the ones who might have been . . .

BALLADEER:

There are those who love regretting,
There are those who like extremes,
There are those who thrive on chaos
And despair.
There are those who keep forgetting
That the country's built on dreams—

ASSASSINS:

People listen . . .

BALLADEER:

And the mailman won the lottery—

ASSASSINS:

They may not want to hear it,
But they listen,
Once they think it's gonna stop the game . . .

BALLADEER:

And the usherette's a rock star—

ASSASSINS:

No, they may not understand
All the words,
All the same

They hear the music . . .
They hear the screams . . .

BALLADEER *(To the Assassins)*:
I've got news—

ASSASSINS:
They hear the sobs,
They hear the drums . . .

BALLADEER:
You forgot about the country—

ASSASSINS:
The muffled drums,
The muffled dreams . . .

BALLADEER:
So it's now forgotten you—

ASSASSINS:
And they rise . . .

BYCK: You know why I did it? Because there isn't any Santa Claus!

ASSASSINS:
Where's my prize?

BALLADEER:
And you forgot—

ASSASSINS:
What's my prize?
BALLADEER:
How quick it heals—

ASSASSINS:
Promises and lies . . .

BALLADEER:
> That it's a place
> Where you can make the lies come true—

ASSASSINS:
> Spread the word . . .

BALLADEER:
> If you try—

ASSASSINS:
> Gotta spread the word . . .

BALLADEER:
> That's all you have to do—

ASSASSINS:
> Right,
> All you have to do . . .

(They advance on the Balladeer, forcing him off the stage. They turn front)

Well, there's another national anthem,
And I think it just began
In the ball park.
Listen hard . . .

Like the other national anthem
Says to each and every fan:
If you can't do what you want to,
Then you do the things you can.
You've got to try again!

GROUP I:
> Like they say—

GROUP II:
> You've got to keep on trying . . .

GROUP I:

Every day—

GROUP II:

Until you get a prize . . .

ALL:

Until you get a prize . . .

(One by one, they start to disappear into the darkness)

GROUP I:

Until you're heard . . .

GROUP II:

Mustn't get discouraged . . .

GROUP I:

Spread the word . . .

GROUP II:

Mustn't give up hope . . .

(Their voices fade into the distance until only the snare drum is faintly heard)

GROUP I:

Up to you—

GROUP II:

Don't say—

GROUP I:

—What you choose . . .

GROUP II:

—It's never gonna happen . . .

GROUP I:

Spread the word . . .

ALL:
> You can always get a prize . . .
> You can always get your dream . . .

BYCK *(Shrugs, the last to disappear)*:
> Sure, the mailman won the lottery . . .

> *(Music dissolves into a country-and-western ballad, as lights come up on . . .)*

SCENE 16

A storeroom on the sixth floor of the Texas School Book Depository in Dallas, Texas. The room is cavernous, with grimy floor-to-ceiling windows. It is filled with schoolbooks, some in cartons, neatly stacked, others set out on metal shelves. There is a clock on the wall and, somewhere on a carton or a shelf, a radio, through which we hear the country-and-western music.

Lee Harvey Oswald, dressed in faded jeans and a tattered T-shirt, sits on a carton reading a handwritten note. On the floor beside him are a lunch pail and a long package wrapped in a blanket. The song on the radio ends. Oswald puts down the note and crosses to the radio as an Announcer comes on.

RADIO ANNOUNCER: That was the Blue Ridge Boys and "Heartache Serenade." And now we take you live to KTEX reporter Harry—

(Oswald turns off the radio and crosses back to the note. He re-reads it. Then he opens the lunch pail, takes out a gun and puts it to his head. From behind one of the bookshelves, we hear whistling—Booth's song from Scene Two. Oswald spins around. John Wilkes Booth steps out into the room)

BOOTH: Oh! I'm sorry. I was just browsing. Please, carry on with whatever you were—

(Booth registers the gun. Oswald looks at it, flushes and shoves it back in the lunch pail. Booth indicates the clock)

Is that the right time? Yes?

(Taking out a pocket watch)

I don't know what's the matter with this thing. Excuse me for a moment—

(Booth crosses to the radio and turns it on)

RADIO ANNOUNCER: —speaking to you from Love Field, where the President's plane has just touched down and is taxiing toward us across the tarmac. We understand the President intends to speak briefly here at the airport before proceeding into Dallas, where—

(Oswald stalks over to the radio and snaps it off. As he does, Booth picks up the note, reads)

BOOTH: Dearest Marina. Today I end my life so that your life can begin. Last night you said that I oppressed you, that—

(Oswald races back, snatches the note)

I'm sorry, is that yours?

OSWALD: Fuck you.

BOOTH: We seem to have gotten off on the wrong foot here. It's my fault. I shouldn't—

(Oswald grabs his lunch pail)

You're not going, are you?

(Oswald heads for the door)

Don't leave now. Come on, I didn't mean to—*Alik.*

(Oswald stops)

OSWALD: What did you call me?

BOOTH: Alik. You used to like that nickname. Back in Minsk. Marina said Lee sounded Chinese, so she called you Alik. Of course *I* don't have to call you Alik. I just thought—

OSWALD: How do you know what Marina called me?

BOOTH: I know lots about you, Lee. Let's see . . . *(Rattling it off like a resume)* Born, New Orleans, October 18, 1939. Father, Robert, died before your birth. Crazy mother, Marguerite. Dropped out of school at seventeen. Joined the Marines. Court-martialed twice. Defected to the Soviet Union, October, 1959. Defected back, June, 1962. Married, Marina Nikolaevna. Two children, June and Rachel. Current employment, stock boy, Texas School Book Depository, Dallas, Texas . . . Oh. And this morning, depressed over your estrangement from a wife who views you as a dismal and pathetic failure, you rose before dawn, kissed your sleeping children, put your last hundred dollars and your wedding ring into a demitasse cup which Marina's mother gave you for a wedding present, and came here to kill yourself . . .

OSWALD: Who are you?

BOOTH: I'm your friend, Lee.

OSWALD: I don't have any friends.

BOOTH: Yes, you do. You just haven't met them yet.

(A beat)

OSWALD: Show me your badge.

BOOTH: My what?

OSWALD: You bastards think you're so smart. I know my rights. You try to interrogate me at my place of business I can sue you for harassment. I can—

BOOTH: Ah! You think I'm with the FBI!

OSWALD: I have a right to see your badge.

(Booth opens his coat, holds out his arms)

BOOTH: Search me, Lee. You think I've got a badge. Come on, search me.

(A beat, then Oswald starts to frisk him. Booth grins)

The FBI. You really love those morons, don't you? Hell, why wouldn't you? No one else cares if you live or die, those guys can't get enough of you. "How was your day, Lee? Sell any secrets to the Soviets? Sabotage any defense plants? Kick off your shoes and tell us all about it!"

OSWALD *(Shoving him away)*: Fuck you, whoever you are!

(Booth smiles)

BOOTH: Lee. I'm sorry, Lee. It's just so sad . . . I mean, it's all you ever wanted, isn't it? Someone who won't leave you alone. Someone who wants to hear about your day. Someone, *anyone*—your mother. Mother Russia. The Marines. Your wife Marina . . . *(He shakes his head)* Attention must be paid.

OSWALD: What's that mean?

BOOTH: It's from a play. About a salesman. A man very much like you, Lee. Independent, proud, a decent man who tries and tries but never gets a break. So he does something dumb. When things go really sour, when he realizes his whole life has been a failure built on lies, he kills himself. And when he's dead, his wife stands at his grave and says attention must be paid. She has to beg the world to pay attention to this poor, misguided nobody . . . I'll tell you something, I'm an actor, Lee. And I'm a good one. But Willy Loman is a part that I could never play. And I don't think that you should play it either.

(A beat)

OSWALD: I don't know what you're talking about.

BOOTH: What do you want, Lee?

OSWALD: You know so much, why don't you tell me?

BOOTH: You want what everybody wants. To be appreciated. To be valued. To be in other people's thoughts. For them to think of you and smile . . . You want someone to love you, Lee. Right? . . . Isn't that it? . . . Lee?

OSWALD: Yes.

BOOTH: Forget it.

OSWALD: What?

BOOTH: It's never going to happen. It's a fantasy. You've got to give it up.

OSWALD: I'm going to kill myself! Don't you think I've given it up?!

BOOTH: No. I think you're going to kill yourself because you think that's how to get it. "When I'm dead, then they'll be sorry! When I'm dead they'll know how much they loved me!" When you close your eyes you probably see the funeral, don't you, Lee? A gentle rain is falling. Everybody has umbrellas—

OSWALD: Shut up!

BOOTH: There's Marina, weeping quietly. Your sobbing children clutching at her skirt. Your mom, your dad. Every boss who ever fired you—

OSWALD: *Shut the fuck up!*

BOOTH: I'm sorry, Lee. It's just so *childish*. It's so *dumb*—

OSWALD: You think it's *dumb*?! If I shouldn't kill myself what *should* I do?! Go home?! Beg her to take me back?! Plead with her?! Beat her up?!

BOOTH: You tried all that. It doesn't work.

OSWALD: I know it doesn't work! So tell me what I *should* do!

BOOTH: You should kill the President of the United States.

OSWALD: What?

BOOTH: His plane landed at the airport fifteen minutes ago. He's coming into town to make a speech. His motorcade is going to go right past this window. When it does, you shoot him.

OSWALD: You're nuts.

BOOTH: Maybe I am. So what?

OSWALD: I didn't come here to shoot the President.

BOOTH: He didn't come here to get shot . . . All your life you've been a victim, Lee. A victim of indifference and neglect. Of your mother's scorn, your wife's contempt, of Soviet stupidity, American injustice. You've finally had enough, so how are you planning to get even? By becoming your *own* victim.

OSWALD: I'm not a murderer.

BOOTH: Who said you were?

OSWALD: You just said I should kill the President. .

BOOTH: Lee, when you kill a President, it isn't murder. Murder is a tawdry little crime; it's born of greed, or lust, or liquor. Adulterers and shopkeepers get murdered. But when a President gets killed, when Julius Caesar got killed . . . he was assassinated. And the man who did it . . . *(He lets the sentence hang, unfinished)*

OSWALD: Brutus.

BOOTH: Ah! You know his name. Brutus assassinated Caesar, what?, two thousand years ago, and here's a high school drop-out with a dollar twenty-five an hour job in Dallas, Texas who knows who he was. And they say fame is fleeting . . .

(He smiles at Oswald; Oswald stares at him. A beat)

OSWALD: This is stupid. Up here on the sixth floor, what would I do? Throw schoolbooks at him?

BOOTH: What's in the package?

OSWALD: What package?

BOOTH *(Indicating package wrapped in blanket)*: The package that you brought to work. What's in it?

OSWALD: Curtain rods.

BOOTH *(Picking up the package)*: You sure?

OSWALD: Sure I'm sure. Marina wanted me to take them to the—

(Booth tosses the package to Oswald; Oswald catches it, looks surprised. He folds back the blanket, revealing a high powered rifle)

BOOTH: That's a Mannlicher-Carcano. 6.5 millimeter. Stopping range, nine hundred yards. The sight's already been adjusted.

OSWALD: Who are you?

BOOTH: My name is John Wilkes Booth, Lee.

OSWALD: John Wilkes Booth shot Abraham Lincoln.

BOOTH *(Quietly, smiling)*: Attention has been paid . . . All your life you've wanted to be part of something, Lee. You're finally going to get your wish.

(Booth gestures. As one, the Assassins from the previous scenes step out from behind the bookshelves: Guiteau, Czolgosz, Zangara, Fromme, Moore, Byck and Hinckley)

OSWALD: What is this?

BOOTH: The past you never had, the future you'd abandoned—it's called history, Lee.

GUITEAU: My name is Charles Guiteau. I assassinated President James Garfield.

CZOLGOSZ: Leon Czolgosz. William McKinley.

BYCK: Sam Byck. I'm going to try to kill Dick Nixon.

HINCKLEY: John Hinckley. Ronald Reagan.

FROMME: Lynette Fromme—

MOORE: Sara Jane Moore—

FROMME, MOORE: Gerald Ford.

ZANGARA: Zangara. FDR.

(A beat)

OSWALD: I don't get this—

MOORE: It's simple, Lee.

CZOLGOSZ *(Indicating pre-Oswald Assassins)*: You're going to bring us back.

HINCKLEY *(Indicating post-Oswald Assassins)*: And make us possible.

GUITEAU: We're in your debt, old boy.

BYCK: This Bud's for you, babe.

GUITEAU: Bravo!

(The Assassins applaud. They start to crowd in around Oswald, patting him on the back, reaching for his hand. He shoves them back, throws down the rifle and grabs his lunch pail)

HINCKLEY *(To Booth)*: What's he doing?

OSWALD: Getting out of here.

GUITEAU: You mean you're not going to do it?

OSWALD: Goddamn right.

(The Assassins explode, some groaning with disappointment, others panicking; to Booth)

GUITEAU: He's not going to do it!

FROMME *(Overlapping)*: You said he would!

HINCKLEY *(Overlapping)*: You promised!

BOOTH: O.K., O.K., shhh . . . Lee, I'm sorry. I know things are happening kind of fast here. But you can't leave now.

OSWALD: No? Watch me—

(Oswald heads for the door)

BOOTH: You have a responsibility here, Lee.

OSWALD: To who? To you?

(A chorus of "yes's" from the Assassins)

I'm responsible to *me* and no one else!

BOOTH: Not anymore, Lee. Fifty years from now they'll still be arguing about the grassy knoll, the mafia, some Cuban crouched behind a stockade fence, but this—right here, right now—this is the real conspiracy. And you're a part of it.

OSWALD: Get out of my way.

BOOTH *(Holding his ground)*: Listen to me, Lee. You have to do this. Now. You won't get another chance.

OSWALD: So what? So I'll do something else. I'll shoot my wife. I'll shoot my kids. I won't shoot anyone! Who cares?!

BOOTH: He wants to know who cares— *(Exploding)* I care, you stupid fool! We *all* care! Haven't you been *listening*, for Christ's sake?! Are you such a vapid, vacuous *nonentity*—

(The Assassins make a quiet "shushing" sound. A beat)

Sorry. I'm sorry . . . John—

97

HINCKLEY: Yes, sir?

BOOTH: John, when Lee was eight he had a dog. What was its name?

HINCKLEY: Tex.

BOOTH: The Marines sent him to radar school. Where?

HINCKLEY: The Naval Air Station, Jacksonville, Florida.

BOOTH: The KGB official who debriefed him in the Kremlin— what was his name and rank?

HINCKLEY: Lieutenant-Colonel Boris Kutzov.

BOOTH: Eighteen years from now, when John tries to assassinate President Reagan, they're going to search his room, and you know what they're going to find? Every book about you ever written.

HINCKLEY *(To Oswald)*: Can I have your autograph?

(Booth gestures to the window)

BOOTH: Take a look, Lee. *(Indicating scene outside)* You know what that is? That's America. The Land Where Any Kid Can Grow Up to Be President. The Shining City, Lee. It shines so bright you have to shade your eyes . . . But in here, this is America, too . . . "The mass of men lead lives of quiet desperation." An American said that. And he was right. But let me tell you something. There are no lives of quiet desperation here. Desperation, yes. But quiet? I don't think so. Not today. Today we're going to make a joyful noise. This is the big one. *You're* the big one. You're the one that's going to sum it all up and blow it all wide open. Why, after you . . .

(He pauses)

GUITEAU: Tell him.

BOOTH: Should I tell him?

ASSASSINS *(Variously)*: Go on! . . . Tell him! . . . Go ahead!

BOOTH: What the hell . . . Is Artie Bremer here tonight? Where's Artie Bremer?!

BREMER'S VOICE *(From somewhere in the house)*: It was a bum rap! My penis made me do it!

(Assassins react; some laugh, Moore shrieks with embarrassment)

BOOTH: Who's next?! Who else is out there?!

VOICE FROM THE HOUSE: Death to the enemies of Palestine!

BOOTH: Of course, of course! Sirhan Sirhan!

(A rebel yell from someplace else in the house)

And James Earl Ray!

(The Assassins give a rebel yell)

Why do these rednecks always have three names? James Earl Ray! John Wilkes Booth—!

OSWALD: —Lee Harvey Oswald!

(The Assassins turn and stare at Oswald; a beat)

BOOTH: I've seen the future, Lee. And you are it.

(Booth snaps his fingers; the radio comes on)

RADIO ANNOUNCER: —and now the motorcade is turning into Elm Street. There's someone holding up a banner, "All the Way with JFK." The President is smiling and waving as his car heads for Dealy Plaza where it will swing past the Texas Book Depository and on to the Trade Mart—

(Booth snaps his fingers again; the radio goes off. He opens the window. From outside, faint sounds of cheers and sirens, gradually growing louder. He holds out the gun)

OSWALD: People will hate me.

BOOTH: They'll hate you with a passion, Lee. Imagine people having passionate feelings about Lee Harvey Oswald . . .

(Oswald reaches for the gun. He hesitates, then drops his hand)

Somebody. Help me . . .

(The Assassins look at one another. A beat, then Zangara steps forward. He speaks in Italian, not in anger, but with passion. The Assassins translate. Music under—a single note)

MOORE *(Translating)*: Please. I beseech you—
CZOLGOSZ *(Translating)*: We are the hopeless ones. The lost ones . . .
GUITEAU *(Translating)*: We live our lives in exile . . .
BYCK *(Translating)*: Expatriates in our own country . . .
HINCKLEY *(Translating)*: We drift from birth to death, despairing . . .
FROMME *(Translating)*: Inconsolable . . .
GUITEAU *(Translating)*: But through you and your act, we dare to hope . . .
MOORE *(Translating)*: Through you and your act we are revived and given meaning . . .
CZOLGOSZ *(Translating)*: Our lives, our acts, are given meaning . . .
HINCKLEY *(Translating)*: Our frustrations fall away . . .
BYCK *(Translating)*: Our fondest dreams come true . . .
FROMME *(Translating)*: Today we are reborn, through you . . .
BOOTH: We need you, Lee.
MOORE: Without you, we're just footnotes in a history book.
GUITEAU: "Disappointed office seeker."
CZOLGOSZ: "Deranged immigrant."
BOOTH: "Vainglorious actor."
FROMME: Without you we're a bunch of freaks.
HINCKLEY: With you we're a force of history.
GUITEAU: We become immortal.
ZANGARA: Finally, we belong.
MOORE: To one another.
CZOLGOSZ: To the nation.
GUITEAU: To the ages.
BYCK: Bring us together, babe.
MOORE: You think you can't connect. Connect to us.

100

CZOLGOSZ: You think you're powerless. Empower us.

BOOTH: It's in your grasp, Lee. All you have to do is move your little finger—you can close the New York Stock Exchange.

GUITEAU: Shut down the schools in Indonesia.

MOORE: In Florence, Italy, a woman will leap from the Duomo clutching a picture of your victim and cursing your name—

CZOLGOSZ: Your wife will weep—

FROMME: His wife will weep—

ZANGARA: The world will weep—

GUITEAU: Grief. Grief beyond imagining—

HINCKLEY: Despair—

MOORE: The death of innocence and hope—

CZOLGOSZ: The bitter burdens which you bear—

BYCK: The bitter truths you carry in your heart—

GUITEAU: You can share them with the world.

BOOTH: You have the power of Pandora's Box, Lee. Open it . . .

(He holds out the gun. Oswald takes it. Music builds underneath as the Assassins sing)

GUITEAU:
 I envy you . . .

MOORE:
 We're your family . . .

HINCKLEY:
 I admire you . . .

CZOLGOSZ:
 I respect you . . .

MOORE:
 Make us proud of you . . .

BOOTH:
 I envy you . . .

GUITEAU:
>   We're your family . . .

>   *(The voices repeat and overlap, mounting in intensity)*

HINCKLEY:
>   I admire you . . .

FROMME, MOORE:
>   We're depending on you . . .

ZANGARA:
>   You are the future . . .

GUITEAU, MOORE:
>   We're your family . . .

CZOLGOSZ:
>   We respect you . . .

BYCK, GUITEAU:
>   Make them listen to us,
>   We've been waiting for you.

BYCK, ZANGARA:
>   Make them listen, boy. . .

>   *(During the above, Oswald has turned and crouched at the window. Urgently, the voices rise)*

ALL *(Variously)*:
>   We admire you . . .
>   We're your family . . .
>   You are the future . . .
>   We're depending on you . . .
>   Make us proud . . .

>   All you have to do is squeeze your little finger.
>   Squeeze your little finger . . .
>   You can change the wor—

(Oswald fires. Music stops for a moment, then resumes, loud, triumphant. Silently, the Assassins exit. Oswald turns. Where did they go? He lurches to his feet, takes his lunch pail and exits. Music dims. A beat, then Booth returns. He picks up Oswald's suicide note, takes matches from his pocket and burns it. As he does, the Book Depository disappears and a slide is projected upstage: the famous photo of Oswald being shot by Jack Ruby. As the photo fades to black, the music changes to a quiet beat . . .)

SCENE 17

Limbo. One by one, the Assassins reappear.

BOOTH *(Sings)*:
    Everybody's
    Got the right
    To be happy.
    Don't be mad,
    Life's not as bad
    As it seems.

CZOLGOSZ:
    If you keep your goal in sight,
    You can climb to any height—

BOOTH, CZOLGOSZ:
    Everybody's
    Got the right
    To their dreams.

MOORE:
    Everybody's
    Got the right
    To be different—

BOOTH, CZOLGOSZ:
    If you want to be different . . .

GUITEAU:
> Even though
> At times they go
> To extremes—

BOOTH, CZOLGOSZ, MOORE:
> Go to extremes . . .

ZANGARA:
> Anybody can prevail—

BYCK:
> Everybody's free to fail—

ALL SIX:
> No one can be put in jail
> For their dreams . . .

ALL:
> Free country—!

HINCKLEY:
> Means that you've got the choice:

GUITEAU:
> Be a scholar!

BYCK:
> Make a dollar!

ALL:
> Free country—!

CZOLGOSZ:
> Means that you get a voice.

ZANGARA:
> Scream and holler!

FROMME:

> Grab 'em by the collar!

ALL:

> Free country—!

OSWALD:

> Means you get to connect!

MOORE, FROMME:

> That's it!

ALL:

> Means the right to expect
> That you'll have an effect,
> That you're gonna connect—

(Advancing, guns at their sides)

> Connect.
> Connect!
> *Connect!*

GROUP *(High voices)*:

> Everybody's
> Got the right
> To some sunshine—

GROUP *(Low voices)*:

> Not the sun,
> But maybe one
> Of its beams.

GROUP *(High voices)*:

> One of its beams . . .

ALL:

> Rich man, poor man,
> Black or white,
> Everybody

Gets a bite,
Everybody
Just hold tight
To your dreams—

Everybody's
Got the right
To their dreams . . .'

*(Pause; final chord as all the guns go off—*BLAM*!—then*
blackout)